BULLETIN OF THE UNIVERSITY OF WISCONSIN

Serial No. 992, General Series No. 776

PIGMENTS OF FLOWERING PLANTS

NELLIE A. WAKEMAN

THESIS SUBMITTED FOR THE DEGREE OF DOCTOR OF PHILOSOPHY
UNIVERSITY OF WISCONSIN
1913

CONTENTS

I. INTRODUCTORY CHAPTER—Theories of color in organic compounds, 7

II. PREFACE, 17

III. PIGMENTS REFERABLE TO HYDROCARBONS OF THE FORMULA OF SATURATION C_nH_{2n-4}, 23

1. Pigments referable to dihydrobenzene, 23
    - Quinone
2. Pigments referable to dihydrotoluene, 24
    - Methyl quinone
3. Pigments referable to dihydrocymene, 24
    - Thymoquinone
    - Monohydroxy thymoquinone
    - Dihydroxy thymoquinone

IV. PIGMENTS REFERABLE TO HYDROCARBONS OF THE FORMULA OF SATURATION C_nH_{2n-6}, 35

1. Pigments referable to benzene, 35
    - Hydroquinone
2. Pigments referable to toluene, 36
    - Hydrotoluquinone
    - Orcinol
3. Pigments referable to o-xylene, 38
    - Orsellinic acid
4. Pigments referable to p-xylene, 37
    - Methyl orcinol
5. Pigments referable to cymene, 38
    - Hydrothymoquinone

V. PIGMENTS REFERABLE TO HYDROCARBONS OF THE FORMULA OF SATURATION C_nH_{2n-8}, 39

1. Pigments referable to phenyl ethene, 39
    - Indican
2. Pigments referable to allyl benzene, 40
    - Daphnetin
    - Aesculetin
    - Scopoletin
    - Fraxetin

VI. PIGMENTS REFERABLE TO HYDROCARBONS OF THE FORMULA OF SATURATION C_nH_{2n-10}, 42

1. Pigments referable to dihydro naphthalene, 42
    - Juglone
2. Pigments referable to methyl dihydro naphthalene, 43
    - Dihydroxy methyl naphthaquinone
    - Trihydroxy methyl naphthaquinone
3. Pigments referable to di-dihydrophenyl ethane, 44
    - Phoeniceine

VII. PIGMENTS REFERABLE TO HYDROCARBONS OF THE FORMULA OF SATURATION C_nH_{2n-12}, 45

1. Pigments referable to naphthalene, 45
    - α Hydrojuglone
    - β Hydrojuglone
2. Pigments referable to methyl 2, butylene 2, dihydro naphthalene, 46
    - Lapachol
3. Pigments referable to methyl 2, butylene 3, dihydro naphthalene, 46
    - Lomatiol

4. Pigments referable to phenyl-dihydro phenyl methane, 47
Rhamnocitrin
β-Rhamnocitrin
VIII. PIGMENTS REFERABLE TO HYDROCARBONS OF THE FORMULA OF SATURATION C_nH_{2n-14}, 48
1. Pigments referable to the diphenyl series of hydrocarbons, 49
a. Pigments referable to ditolyl
Ellagic acid
2. Pigments referable to diphenyl methane series of hydrocarbons and their homologues, 50
a. Pigments referable to diphenyl methane, 51
Cotoin
Euxanthone
Euxanthonic acid
Maclurin
Kenoin
Gentiseine
Gentisin
Datiscetin
b. Pigments referable to phenylethophenyl methane, 58
Catechin
Cyanomaclurin
c. Pigments referable to diphenyl ethane, 62
Genistein
d. Pigments referable to diphenyl propane, 62
Phloretin
Butin
Saponarin
Vitexin
IX. PIGMENTS REFERABLE TO HYDROCARBONS OF THE FORMULA OF SATURATION C_nH_{2n-16}, 67
1. Pigments referable to hydrocarbons of the diphenyl olefin series, 68
a. Pigments referable to diphenyl ethene series, 69
a. Pigments referable to tolyl-ethophenyl-ethene, 69
Berberin
b. Pigments referable to diphenyl 1, 3, propene, 71
b' Flavone derivatives, 76
Chrysin
Tectochrysin
Apiginin
Acacetin
Galangin
Galangin methyl ether
Luteolin
Luteolin methyl ether
Lotoflavin
Fisetin
Kaempherol
Kaempherid
Quercetin
Rhamnetin
Irorhamnetin
Rhamnazin
Morin
Myricetin
Gossypelin

b″ Butein, 98
b‴ Anthocyanins, 99
Pelargonidin
Cyanidin
Paeonidin
Delphinidin
Myrtillidin
Malvidin
Oenidin
c. Pigments referable to 1, 4, butene 2.
Indigotin
2. Pigments referable to dihydroanthracene and its homologues, 110
a. Pigments referable to dihydroanthracene, 116
Hydroxy-2-anthraquinone
Alizarin
Hystazarin
Xanthopurpurin
Anthragallol
Purpurin
b. Pigments referable to methyl-1-anthracene, 123
Rubiadin
Chrysophanic acid
Emodin
Aloemodin
Rhein
c. Pigments referable to methyl-2-anthracene, 129
Morindon
Psuedopurpurin
3. Pigments referable to methyl-phenyl-hydrindine and their oxidation products, 131
a. Derivatives of methyl-phenyl-hydrindine, 132
Brasilin
Haematoxlyn
b. Oxidation products of methyl-phenyl-hydrindine, 134
Brasilein
Haematein
X. Pigments Referable to Hydrocarbons of the Formula of Saturation C_nH_{2n-18}, 136
1. Pigments referable to hydrocarbons with nine double bonds and one cycle, 136
The Chlorophylls
2. Pigments referable to hydrocarbons with eight double bonds and two cycles, 139
Curcumine
3. Pigments referable to hydrocarbons with seven double bonds and three cycles, 142
Trifoletin
4. Pigments referable to hydrocarbons with six double bonds and four cycles, 143
Chrysarobin
XI. Pigments Referable to Hydrocarbons of the Formula of Saturation C_nH_{2n-24}, 144
Carotin
Lycopin
Xanthophyll
XII. Pigments Referable to Hydrocarbons of the Formula of Saturation C_nH_{2n-34}, 145
Di(methyl-dihyro anthracyl)

Errata

Page 16. In the first fluorescein formula two carbon atoms have been omitted by the printer.

Page 46. The formula for methyl-2-butylene-3-dihydronaphthalene contains an unnecessary "C".

Page 73. In Kostanecki's formula for flavone, the numbers 1 to 4 of the chromone group should be devoid of primes.

Page 87. In the formula for Kaempherid the hydrogen atom in position 3 should be replaced by a hydroxy group.

Page 120. In the anthragallol dimethyl ether A formula the treble bond between two of the carbon atoms should be replaced by a double bond.

Page 133. Haematoxylin for Haematoxlyn.

Page 134. In the formula for β-methyl-γ-phenyl isohydrindine the seemingly trivalent carbon atom should have an additional hydrogen atom.

Page 138. In the formula for aetiophyllin, the seemingly tetravalent nitrogen and pentavalent carbon atoms should be united by a single bond.

PIGMENTS OF FLOWERING PLANTS.

INTRODUCTORY CHAPTER.

THEORIES OF COLOR IN ORGANIC COMPOUNDS.

While the study of pigmentation in plants early attracted the attention of chemists as well as botanists, it was not until the introduction of synthetic dye stuffs in the latter part of the 19th century that any considerable amount of attention was directed to the determination of the cause of color in the pigment itself. Until this time indeed, the constitution of most of the natural dye stuffs was unknown, consequently any consideration of the relationship between color and molecular structure was impossible. With the introduction of dye stuffs of known constitution, however, the question not only presented itself but well nigh forced itself upon the attention of chemists. The earlier endeavors were, for the most part, directed toward determining a direct relationship between color and molecular constitution. This led to a study of so-called chromophorous groups and chromogens, a study which, while it has been fruitful of results in the manufacture of dye stuffs, has been of much less value in the study of plant pigments. Recently, however, these studies have assumed a more basal character and the subject has been approached through the general question of absorption spectra, the invisible as well as the visible portion of the spectrum being taken into consideration.

It is obvious that color does not inhere in the colored substance itself, but is the response of sensation to the stimulus of light which proceeds from the colored substance either by transmission or reflection. The different dyes and pigments possess their many varying hues because, by a process known as selective absorption, each pigment absorbs certain definite colors from white light and transmits or reflects only those which it does not absorb. A transparent object takes on the color of the light which it transmits, while an opaque object takes on that of the light which it reflects.* If an object absorbs all of the radiations of white light and transmits none, it is black; if it absorbs all but the red radiations, for example, it is red; but if it absorbs none and transmits all of the radiations of white light, it appears to be colorless. Again, if light of only one color be absorbed, violet for example, its complementary color, yellow in this instance, will alone be visible. If on the other hand two complementary colors alone are absorbed, the object will appear relatively colorless. Many substances are quite transparent and colorless within the limits of the visible spectrum which show selective absorption in the infra-red or ultra-violet regions. Such substances only appear colorless. In a physical sense they are similar to colored substances, for, physically, there is little difference whether absorption is of radiant energy of short wave length in the ultra violet, of medium wave length in the visible portion of the spectrum, or of long wave length in the infra-red.

That a substance shows selective absorption is probably due to the fact that the oscillation frequencies of its molecules correspond to certain definite wave lengths of radiant energy, the energy corresponding to such wave lengths being absorbed by the molecules. In accordance with this theory of color in material objects, much attention has been paid in recent years to the question of what molecular structures are likely to correspond to more or less definite periods of molecular vibrations, thus producing selective absorption. Narrowed down to the study of pigments, the question has taken the form of what particular configurations, as well as the introduction of what group or groups of elements, will throw this selective absorption into the region of the visible spectrum where color will be produced. This brings the whole subject of chromophorous groups into a new light and explains how the introduction of a given group, supposed to aid in the production

* Comparatively few substances, e. g. the metals, some solid organic dyes, feathers, etc., which have a metallic lustre, owe their color to reflection. Most substances generally considered opaque transmit light for some distance below the surface. Color in such substances is a transmission rather than reflection phenomenon.

of color, might result in one case in the change of a colorless substance to a colored one, while in another case it might have the opposite result of taking away the color from a colored substance. It shows, in fact, that color in a substance is not a function of a particular group of elements but of the structure of the entire molecule.

The first attempt to show the relationship between constitution and color in organic compounds appears to have been that of Graebe and Liebermann[1] in 1868. These investigators laid down the rule as of general application that, if the colored metallic salts of colorless organic acids are excepted, all colored organic compounds are rendered colorless by reducing agents, and that in this reduction the compound adds on hydrogen without the elimination of any other elements from the molecule. As illustrations they quote quinone, $C_6H_4\left\{\begin{matrix}O\\O\end{matrix}\right\rangle$ reduced to hydroquinone, $C_6H_6\left\}\begin{matrix}OH\\OH\end{matrix}\right.$; azobenzene, $C_6H_5\,N{=}N{-}C_6H_5$; reduced to hydrazobenzene, $C_6H_5\,\underset{H}{N}{-}\underset{H}{N}{-}C_6H_5$, etc.

From these reactions they infer that colored compounds either contain elements with incompletely saturated affinities, or that some of the atoms are more intimately bound than is necessary for their retention in the molecule; furthermore, that the physical property of color depends upon the manner in which the oxygen or nitrogen atom is combined, in the colored compounds these elements being in more intimate combination than in the colorless compounds. In the case of colored nitro and nitroso compounds, which are rendered colorless by reduction to amido compounds, it is the intimate association of the oxygen and nitrogen to form a group which renders the substance colored.

Graebe and Liebermann's theory was formulated before the present diketone formula for quinones was accepted, their conception of a quinone being that of a benzene nucleus with two oxygen atoms linked together, hence the idea of "more intimate, or internal, combination."

In 1876 Witt[2] advanced an entirely different explanation.

[1] Ber., 1, p. 106

[2] Ber., 9, p. 522.

Color in a substance, according to Witt, is due to the presence of a chromophore group in the molecule. Such a substance, though generally colored, is not a dyestuff and is called by Witt a chromogen. It becomes a dye by the introduction of a salt forming auxochrome group. According to Witt the principal chromophore groups are. the nitro $-N\begin{smallmatrix}\nearrow O\\ \searrow O\end{smallmatrix}$, the nitroso, $-N=O$, the carbonyl $-C=O$, and the allied group the thio carbonyl, $=C=S$; and also the azo menthin group $-C=N-$, the azo group $-N=N-$. The principal auxochrome groups are the hydroxyl, the amino, and the mono- and di- alkyl amino groups. Witt's theory, while it proved of great value in the synthesis of artificial dyes, as stated before, has been of comparatively little use in the study of plant pigments, since only the corbonyl group among the so called chromophore groups and the hydroxy among the auxochrome groups are of at all frequent occurrence in the plant pigments of known constitution. Moreover the mere presence of these two groups, or of multiples of one or both, is not sufficient to explain the phenomenon of color in the plant pigment molecule.

From time to time other chromophore groups have been added to those named by Witt. Principal among these are the ethylene[3] group $=C=C=$, the azoxy[4] group $\begin{smallmatrix}-N-N-\\ \diagdown\ \diagup\\ O\end{smallmatrix}$ or $\begin{smallmatrix}-N=N-\\ \|\\ O\end{smallmatrix}$ or $\begin{smallmatrix}-N=N-\\ \diagdown\ \diagup\\ O\end{smallmatrix}$, and combinations of some of the above named groups.

In 1888 Armstrong[5] introduced his quinone theory of color. Since dyestuffs in general can, by the addition of hydrogen, be reduced to the corresponding leuco bases, Armstrong considered all colored compounds to be quinones and the corresponding colorless compounds to be hydroquinones. Using the Fittig diketone formula for quinones, Armstrong attempted to show that the structure of colored compounds in general may be represented by a quinoidal formula. Under the term quinoidal formula Armstrong included all structures containing

[3] Ber., 33, p. 666.
[4] Ber., 31, p. 1361; 33, p. 123; 29, p. 2413.
[5] Proc. Chem. Soc., 4, p. 27; 8, pp. 101, 143, 189, 194.

either the para quinone or the ortho quinone grouping, the double bonds being satisfied by oxygen or any other divalent element or group or by combinations of any of them.

Armstrong's theory has received a great deal of attention, much evidence both for and against it having been produced. Though our present knowledge of the structure of colored compounds would indicate that by no means all colored substances are of quinoidal character, yet a surprisingly large number, if not all, of the substances of a quinoidal configuration are colored. The quinoidal configuration is in fact one of the best known and most reliable chromogens.

In the study of plant pigments the quinone theory has proved of much more value than Witt's theory of chromophorous groups. The constitution and the properties of a very large number of vegetable dyestuffs, and of other colored substances derived from plants, have been accounted for by assuming a quinoidal structure. Moreover the closely related quinhydrone[6] hypothesis of pigmentation in some plants promises to explain biochemically the existence of many colors and shades of color, as well as many changes of color, which have hitherto been unaccounted for.

In considering quinone and quinhydrone hypotheses of pigmentation mention should be made of Richter's[7] oxonium theory of quinones. According to Richter the characteristics of oxonium salts, namely simple addition of the components in their formation, ready decomposition in solution, and upon sublimation, and marked increase in intensity of color, are also those of the quinhydrones. For these and other reasons hydroquinones, phenoquinones, etc., are regarded by Richter as oxonium compounds formed by the addition of pnenols, etc., to the tetravalent oxygen of quinones.

Assuming that the doubly bound oxygen of quinones acts as a tetravalent oxygen does not impair the validity of the quinhydrone hypothesis as suggested by Kremers and Brandel. It brings the quinone pigments into line with the anthocyanin pigments, as interpreted by Willstaetter, and explains how many quinones, as well as many flavone and xanthone derivatives, also haematin and brazilin, dissolve in acids with an in-

[6] Ph. Rev., 19, p. 200.
[7] Ber., 43, p. 3603.

tense color, but are precipitated unchanged from this solution by the addition of water. It is easy to understand how the tetravalent oxygen in quinones, being basic, might add on the elements of phenols as well as acids or how it might add on the elements of a molecule of water. While it would not be wise, however, without very careful investigation, to say it were impossible, it is not easy, without altering our present conception of the tetravalent oxygen, to see how the same oxygen could be able to form addition products with organic nitrogen bases, such as phenylendiamine, and even with potassium hydroxide, which Richter represents it as doing.

In 1879 Nietzki[8] formulated a rule, supposed to be of general application, that the pigments of most simple construction are yellow and by increase of molecular weight they gradually change from yellow to red, then to violet, then to blue.

Schuetze[9] in 1892 found that Nietzki's rule holds only in certain cases; but that changes in color in general are the results of changes in selective absorption in the regions of the visible spectrum. The results of Schuetze's investigations are summed up as follows:

1. A change of absorption from violet toward red usually causes the following changes in color; greenish yellow, yellow, orange, red, reddish violet, violet, bluish violet, blue, bluish green, etc. Passing through the colors in this direction Schuetze calls deepening or lowering the tint; in the opposite direction, raising the tint.

2. Definite atoms and atomic groups by their entrance into the molecule cause, for compounds of the same chromophore in the same solvent, a characteristic deepening or raising of the tint. Those which deepen the tint are called "bathochrome" groups or elements, those which raise the tint are called "hypsochrome" groups or elements.

3. Hydrocarbon radicles are always bathochromic. Consequently in homologous series the shade always deepens as the molecular weight increases.

4. The same deepening of color is caused in the groups of the periodic series as the atomic weights increase.

---

[8] Verhandl. des Vereins fur Befoerderung der Gewerbfleisses., 58, p. 231 (Quoted by Schuetze, Zeit. fur Phys. Chem., 9, p. 109).

[9] Zeit. fur Phys. Chem., 9, p. 109.

5. The addition of hydrogen always results in raising the tint.

6. The rise or fall of the tint (the passage of absorption from violet to red) by substitution of hypsochrome or bathochrome groups, or by the addition or loss of hydrogen, is the greater the nearer the atoms affected by the change are to the chromophore group. From this it would appear that in the bi-derivitives of benzene the substituents in para position are nearer to each other than those in ortho position.

7. These rules hold only for monochromophoric compounds and for symmetrical dichromophoric compounds. The color of an unsymmetrical dichromophoric compound, Y, A, X, A, Z, is approximately the same as that of a mixture of the two symmetrical compounds, Y, A, X, A, Y, and Z, A, X, A, Z.

In general the term bathochrome group is interpreted to mean a group which swings the absorption toward the red, and a hypsochrome group, one which swings the absorption toward the violet. Among the former are the hydrocarbon radicles, the halogens, and the salt forming groups with the exception of the amino group. Among the latter are the acetyl and the benzoyl groups, the alkyl-oxy groups, hydrogen, and the amino group. The sulpho group is sometimes one and sometimes the other.

The effect of the introduction of bathochrome and hypsochrome groups upon the color of the original substance depends upon the original molecule, the position of the group, and the number of groups introduced. It is easy to understand how the introduction of one bathochrome group might deepen the color by throwing the absorption into the red, while the introduction of two or three such groups would remove it by throwing the absorption wholly outside the visible spectrum. Again the same two or three groups might be required to render another molecule colored. Here again we find additional evidence that the color of a substance is not conditioned by the presence of a definite group, or groups, but by the entire structure of the molecule.

In 1904 Baly and Desch[10] in the course of a study of the ultraviolet spectrum of certain enol-keto tautomerides brought forth evidence to support the view that the absorption bands exhibited by these substances are due to the equilibrium existing

[10] Proc. Chem. Soc., 85, p. 1029.

between the two possible tautomeric forms. Neither of the two substances in a pure state exhibits absorption but when the two are present in mutual equilibrium, that is, when a number of molecules are changing from one form to another, a very decided absorption band is formed. In 1905[11] they stated further:

1. No organic substance shows an absorption band unless a possibility for tautomerism exists in the molecule.

2. This tautomerism may not be due to a labile atom, but may be of the same order as that occurring in those aromatic compounds containing the true benzenoid structure.

3. In all cases of the simpler tautomeric molecule the vibration frequencies of the absorption bands are very nearly the same.

4. An increase in the mass of the molecule causes a decrease in the oscillation frequencies of the absorption band, i. e. a shifting toward the red.

Baly and Desch account for these facts and explain the formation of the absorption band by the same theory as that advanced by physicists to explain the phenomena of radio activity, emission spectra, etc., namely the electron theory.

In 1906 Baly and Stewart[12] applied the principle involved in the foregoing to many colored compouds. As a result of their investigations they conclude:

The color of diketones and quinones is due to an oscillation or isorropesis between the residual affinities of the oxygen atoms which results in the absorption of light in the visible spectrum. Also that in order to start the oscillation it is necessary that some influence should be present to disturb the residual affinities of the oxygen atoms. When this disturbing influence is present there is no doubt that the principle may be extended, and that visible color is due to the oscillations between the residual affinities on atoms or groups of atoms in juxtapposition. They also call attention to the fact that the assumption that two compounds must be fundamentally different in constitution if one is colored and the other not is quite untrustworthy. Many compounds can and do exist with all the conditions for isorropesis and yet there is lacking the influence to disturb the equilibrium between the residual affinities and so the com-

---

[11] Proc. Chem. Soc., 87, p. 766.
[12] Jr. Chem. Soc., 89, pp. 502, 514, 966, 982.

pounds are colorless. They consider this principle to be the key to Armstrong' theory of color and as an explanation of the colors of many compounds which are difficult of interpretation by Armstrong's quinoid linking alone, for though Armstrong was perfectly right in concluding that color is due to quinoid linking, this formula gives no reasons why color is thus produced.

In 1907[13] Hale drew practically the same conclusions as those of Baly and his associates, namely that isorropesis is the cause of color in both the aromatic and the aliphatic series. By isorropesis is meant the making and breaking of contact between atoms thus giving them marked activity. This change of linkage which must accompany the transformation of one modification of the compound to the other is the source of the oscillations producing the absorption bands. If these oscillations are synchronous with light waves of a high frequency they give rise to absorption bands in the ultra violet and the compound is colorless. If, however, they are less frequent, the absorption band appears in the visible portion of the spectrum and this absorption of colored rays results in the compound taking on the complementary color.

In 1907 Hewett and Mitchell[14] pointed out that in every case of colored compounds the molecules contain not merely double linkages but chains of alternate double and single linkages. Generally speaking the longer this chain of conjugate double linkages the slower the oscillation frequency of the molecule. This explains why a benzene nucleus gives absorption bands in the ultra violet and is colorless while a quinone nucleus gives absorption bands in the violet and is therefore colored yellow. In estimating the number of such alternate double and single linkages, when a benzene nucleus is encountered, one is justified in following the structure around one side of the ring only until para position is reached. The chain in the benzene nucleus, therefore, contains at best only two double linkages, while that of the quinone contains three.

Hewett and Mitchell also conclude that a radical change in the absorption spectrum of a compound when it undergoes salt formation generally means the radical alteration of its consti-

[13] Pop. Sci. Mo., 72, p. 116.
[14] Jr. Chem. Soc., 91, p. 1251.

tution. Other groups or elements when introduced in place of hydrogen may diminish the oscillation frequency, but the effect in such cases must be slight and the general character of the absortion would remain unaltered. It is conceivable that such groups introduced into the molecule of a substance colorless in the ordinary sense, might, if its absorption occurs just outside the visible spectrum, render the substance colored by a slight shifting of the absorption band; but when a radical change in the color takes place on salt formation the salt is constituted differently from the parent substance.

In 1900 Hewett[15] advanced the idea that symmetrical compounds capable of equal tautomeric displacements in either of two directions should be fluorescent, for the molecule would swing between the two extremes like a pendulum, the energy absorbed in one wave length being degraded and given out with slower frequency.

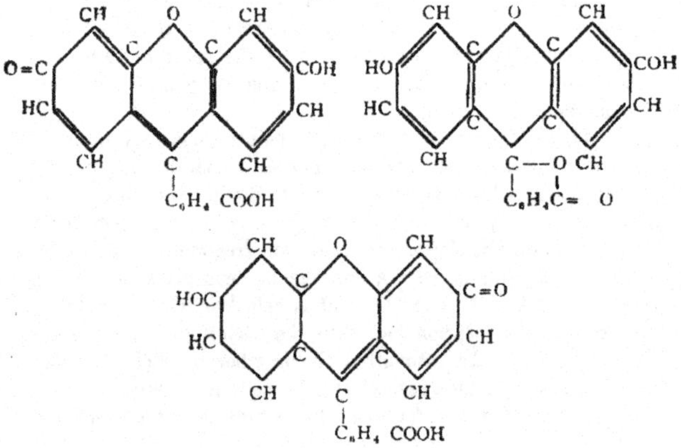

Fluorescein.

In 1910 Porai-Koschitz[16] summed up the more recent views of the oscillation theory of the cause of color in organic compounds as follows: The change in color of a compound is due to the retarding of the oscillations or the setting up of a new

[15] Zeitschr. physikal. Chem., 34, p. 1. (See also Jr. Phys. Chem. 10, p. 375; Jr. Chem. Soc., 87, p. 768.)

[16] Jr. Russ. Phys. Chem. Soc., 42, p. 1237. (Jr. Chem. Soc., A. II, p. 3.)

type of oscillations within the molecule by the entrance of a new group, by the formation of a molecular compound, or by the associations of the molecule of a solute with those of its solvent. Three cases are possible:

1. The new oscillation may coincide with and increase the original oscillation; then the absorption band will move further toward the ultra-violet and the compound will remain, or become visibly colorless.

2. The new oscillation may be an entirely different type from the original, in which case new bands will appear, and since the original oscillation will be retarded to some extent, there will be a change but not a very considerable one in the visible color of the substance.

3. The new oscillation may combine with the original and retard it greatly, when there will be a considerable sharp change in color.

PREFACE.

Work upon plant pigments was begun by the writer during the summer of 1907 when, as an undergraduate student, her attention was directed to pigmentation in the Monarda species. Since that time, though the subject has been sometimes temporarily pushed aside by other interests, it has never been lost sight of and it has usually been the subject of most absorbing interest. At times the work has appeared to be of a purely chemical nature, without any biochemical significance, as in the study of thymoquinone, hydrothymoquinone, and the oxidation products of thymoquinone. Its object at these times has been to elucidate the behavior of certain plant pigments, i. e. those of the Monarda species. Sometimes it has been of a character usual in the study of plant pigments, the extraction of pigments from the plants themselves and an examination of the products obtained. At other times it has been of what is generally considered of a more purely biochemical character, a study of oxidases, water content, etc., and their relation to the formation of pigments in plants.

It has been found in the course of these investigations that no adequate and satisfactory knowledge of plant pigments can be gained by a study of simply the pigments themselves; but that each pigment should be considered not only in relation to the other colored substances in the same and related plants, but also to the non-colored substances as well. A close and peculiar relationship has often been found to exist between the colored and the non-colored constituents not only of the same plant, but sometimes of the related species of a whole plant family.

As the work progressed a complete revision of the literature on plant pigments became necessary. Very little literature of a general nature upon plant pigments was found to exist, almost nothing in fact beyond Brandel's excellent monograph. Several treatises upon vegetable dye stuffs, it is true, are available. Among these may be mentioned two by Thomas, *Les Matiéres Colorantes Naturelles,* and *Les Plantes Tinctoriales,* also Rupe's more recent *Chemie der natuerlichen Farbstoffe* (1909) and volume 6 of the *Biochemisches Hand-Lexicon, Farbstoffe der Pflanzen und der Tierwelt.* (1911), as well as chapters on natural dye stuffs in various treatises on dye stuffs in general. By far the larger literature on plant pigments, however, is scattered through the chemical and botanical journals of the past fifty years, some extending much further back. Before attempting to proceed further with work upon plants and plant products it seemed desirable to review this literature in order,

1. To avoid useless repetition of work already done.
2. To interpret new work in the light of the old, and the old in the light of recent experimentation.
3. To make comparisons, draw conclusions, and formulate theories as a guide to future work.

In the course of this review of the literature upon plant pigments it was found that by arranging the pigments according to the degree of saturation, as calculated from the underlying hydrocarbons, certain relationships were brought out which could not well be observed in any other way. Among the important relationships emphasized by this classification are:

1. The influence of unsaturation upon the production of color in a molecule.
2. The influence of so called chromophorous groups upon the production of color in a molecule.
3. The existence of homologous series of pigments.

4. The existence of series of pigments related to similar symmetrical, or almost symmetrical hydrocarbons of different degrees of saturation.

1. ***The influence of unsaturation upon the production of color in a molecule.***

In this connection it should be pointed out that all organic pigment molecules are unsaturated. The highest degree of saturation known in a pigment molecule is C_nH_{2n-4}, and visible color exists in substances of this degree of saturation only when the quinone grouping is present, the quinone grouping being one of the best known and most reliable of the chromophorous groups.

Among substances referable to hydrocarbons of the degree of saturation C_nH_{2n-6} no substances colored in the ordinary sense are known to exist but several pigment producing substances are known. All substances, however, having a benzenoid grouping are colored in a physical sense, since they all exhibit selective absorption, not, it is true in the visible portion of the spectrum but just beyond it in the ultra violet.

The largest number by far of plant pigments are referable to hydrocarbons of the degrees of saturation C_nH_{2n-14} and C_nH_{2n-16}, though colored substances of known constitution referable to hydrocarbons of higher unsaturation, up to C_nH_{2n-34}, have been isolated from plants. Moreover, all colored hydrocarbons, in which the production of color cannot be attributed to the usual chromophorous groups, are highly unsaturated, caroten and lycopen being of the degree of saturation C_nH_{2n-24}, while the blue hydrocarbon from oil of milfoil, having the formula $C_{15}H_{18}$, is apparently of the degree of saturation C_nH_{2n-12}.

2. *Influence of co-called chromophorous groups upon the production of color.*

As has been pointed out elsewhere in this paper, but little has been contributed to our knowledge of pigmentation in plants by a study of chromophorous groups, since only the corbonyl of the so-called chromophorous groups and the hydroxyl of the auxochrome groups are of at all frequent occurrence in plant pigments. Neither is the mere presence of either or both of these groups, or of multiples of one or both, sufficient to explain the phenomenon of color in any known plant pigment. In many instances, however, the influence of both the presence and the position of these groups, especially of the hydroxy group, is evident. For example, the substitution of hydroxy groups for hydrogen in the xanthone or flavone pigments usually intensifies both the color and the dyeing properties of these substances, while the removal of such groups, either by replacement with hydrogen or by methylation, usually diminishes both. In no instance does the presence of the chromophorous group explain the color. In most cases it will be seen that it is not the mere presence of these so-called chromophorous groups but their relation to each other and to the rest of the molecule which postulates color in a substance. Color, in other words, appears to be a function, not of certain groups or elements but of the entire molecule.

3. *The existence of homologous series of plant pigments,* or more accurately, of pigments referable to homologous series of hydrocarbons is worthy of note. This homology is manifest in connection with every degree of saturation where a sufficiently large number of pigments, or of pigment forming substances, to admit of comparisons adequate to justify the drawing of conclusions, has been isolated.

Under the degree of saturation C_nH_{2n-4} we find evidence of the existence of quinone, methyl quinone and of methyl p-isopropyl quinone. Similarly, under the formula of saturation C_nH_{2n-6} the pigment forming substances hydroquinone, methyl hydroquinone, and methyl-p-isopropl hydroquinone are found. A similar homology is found to exist in connection with pigments referable to hydrocarbons of other degrees of saturation, especially to C_nH_{2n-16} where we find pigments referable to homologues of diphenyl ethene, diphenyl propene, etc., as well as to homologous series of dihydroanthracenes.

A condition quite similar in many respects to homology, and sometimes confused with it, exists among the pigments falling under the degrees of saturation C_nH_{2n-14} and C_nH_{2n-16}. This is the existence of pigments referable to closely related series of hydrocarbons, not truly homologous yet differing from one another by CH_2, such as diphenyl, diphenyl methane, diphenyl ethane, diphenyl propane, among the former; and diphenyl ethene, diphenyl propene, and diphenyl butene among the latter, as well as alkyl substitution products of these hydrocarbons. This relationship is very similar to that existing between pigments referable to hydrocarbons of different degrees of saturation discussed in the following paragraph.

4. *The existence of series of compounds referable to similar symmetrical, or nearly symmetrical hydrocarbons of different degrees of saturation.*

A relationship quite similar to that expressed by homology under the same degree of saturation is noted between the hydrocarbons of different degrees of saturation to which any of the plant pigments are referable. This relationship is best expressed by the accompanying chart of graphic formulae representing the hydrocarbons to which a large majority of the plant pigments falling under the degrees of saturation C_nH_{2n-10} to C_nH_{2n-18} are referable.

In addition to the hydrocarbons listed in this table, attention should here be called to pigments, or pigment forming substances, referable to benzene and dihydrobenzene, naphthalene and dihydronaphthalene anthracene and dihydroanthracene series of hydrocarbons. It is also interesting to note the symmetrical or almost symmetrical character of all of the above hydrocarbons. Whether this symmetry of arrangement of the underlying hydrocarbon is only coincident with the conditions which produce color in the molecule, or whether the symmetrical arrangement is itself one of the conditions does not become manifest.

In order to bring out the relationships just discussed the plant pigments of known constitution have here been classified according to the underlying hydrocarbon. A second classification, according to plant families, showing the relationship which exists between the pigments and the noncolored constituents of the same and related plants, was intended to be included. This classification was, however, found to be too long for the purposes of this paper, therefore will be published later as supplementary to it. The experimental work of the writer[1], where heretofore published has been referred to in the same manner as that of other investigators. Some work not previously published has been briefly described, i. e. the study of the pigment of red geranium blossoms. In addition to the above a large amount of

---

[1] Quantitative determinatino of oxidase in the leaves of Monarda fistulosa.
Ph. Rev., 26, p. 314.
Thymoquinone and Hydrothmoquinone.
Ph. Rev., 26, p. 329.
Higher oxidation products of thymoquinone.
Proc. A. Ph. A., 58, p. 979.
The Monardas, a phytochemical study.
Bull. of Univ. of Wis., Sci. Ser., Vol. 4, No. 4, pp. 81–128.

$C_n H_{2n-10}$	$C_n H_{2n-12}$	$C_n H_{2n-14}$	$C_n H_{2n-16}$	$C_n H_{2n-18}$
		Di phenyl		
$-CH_2-$ **di-dihydro phenyl-methane**	$-CH_2-$ **Phenyl-dihydro phenyl-methane**	$-CH_2-$ **Di phenyl methane**		
		$-CH_2-CH_2-$ **Diphenyl ethane**	$-CH=CH-$ **Diphenyl ethene**	
		$-CH_2-CH_2-CH_2-$ **Diphenyl propane**	$-CH_2-CH=CH-$ **Diphenyl propene**	
			$-CH_2-CH=CH-CH_2-$ **Diphenyl butene**	
				$CH_2 \langle {CH_2-CH=CH- \atop CH_2-CH=CH-}$ **Diphenyl hepta diene**

material has been collected and studied for the purpose of making comparisons and verifying conclusions.

PLANT PIGMENTS.

PIGMENTS REFERABLE TO HYDROCARBONS OF THE FORMULA OF SATURATION C_nH_{2n-4}.

All of the known plant pigments of this degree of saturation are quinones or more particularly their quinhydrone or phenoquinone addition products, and metallic derivatives of the latter, and are referable to dihydro benzene, dihydro toluene and dihydro cymene.

Pigments referable to dihydrobenzene.

H C; HC, CH_2; H_2C, CH; CH

Dihydro benzene

CH; HC, C=O; O=C, CH; C H

Benzo quinone

The only plant pigment referable to dihydro benzene, of whose existence in plants we have any evidence, is the ordinary quinone, or benzoquinone. However, its occurrence is purely hypothetical. Though benzoquinone has never yet been isolated from a plant, its dihydro derivative, hydroquinone, is known to occur in several species and under such conditions as would suggest the formation of quinone and quinhydrone as a possible explanation of the pigmentation which exists there. For example, the glucosides arbutin and methyl arbutin occur in the leaves of *Gaultheria procumbens, Uva ursi,* and several other species of the Ericaceae. Arbutin upon hydrolysis yields hydroquinone. Hydroquinone by the action of oxidases, known to occur in *Gaultheria* and, no doubt, present in the other arbutin containing plants, is readily converted into quinone with the formation of quinhydrone as an intermediate product. The presence of benzoquinhydrone, which is brownish-red in color, would afford an explanation of the reddish tint commonly acquired by the leaves and stems of these plants in the fall. It might also account for the remarkable colorations of the *Madrones* and *Manzanitas* so well known upon the Pacific coast, since both are species of *Arbutus* and closely related to the above named plants. Arbutin has been isolated from the leaves of at least one of the manzanitas, *Arctostaphylos glauca.*

Hydroquinone also exists as the mono methyl ether in the oil of star anise. *Illicium verum*, a member of the family *Magnoliaceae*.[1]

Pigments referable to dihydrotoluene

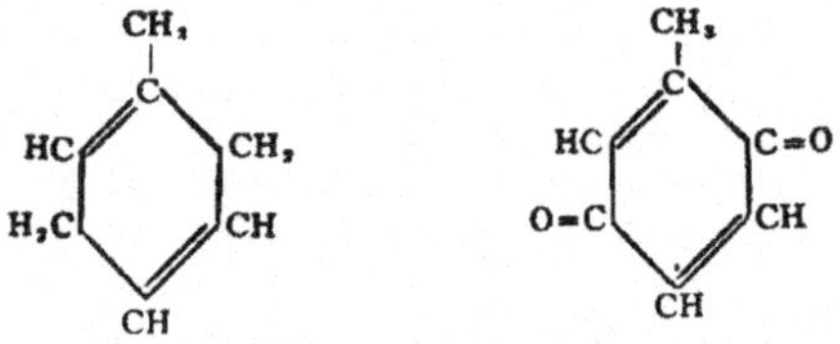

Dihydrotoluene

Methyl benzoquinone

As has been pointed out in connection with quinone, methyl hydroquinone exists potentially in *Gaultheria procumbens* and other species of the *Ericaceae* as the glucoside methyl arbutin. The same possibilities for forming pigments by hydrolysis, oxidation, and addition exist in both quinone and methyl quinone.

Pigments referable to dihydrocymene

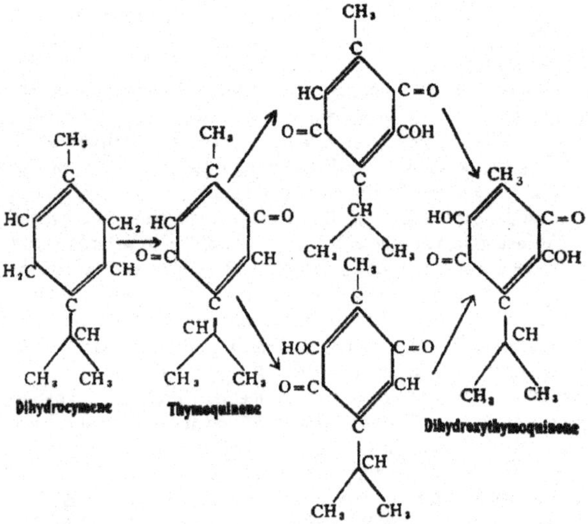

Dihydrocymene

Thymoquinone

Dihydroxythymoquinone

Monohydroxythymoquinones

[1] For references see under Hydroquinone, formula of saturation C_nH_{2n-6}

Of the oxidation products of dihydrocymene, three, and possibly four, are believed to exist in plants. Of these thymoquinone and dihydroxy thymoquinone have actually been isolated, while there are strong reasons for believing that one or both of the monohydroxy thymoquinones occur in *Monarda* species either in the free state or as labile compounds.

Thymoquinone together with the corresponding hydroquinone has been isolated from several species of *Monarda*, also from the oil from the wood of *Thuja articulata.*[2] Hydrothymoquinone also exists in the oil from the fruit of *Foeniculum vulgare*,[3] also as dimethyl ether in the oil of *Eupatorium triplinerve*[4] (*E. Ayapana*) and in the oil from *Eupatorium capillifolium.*[5] Inasmuch as in the diethers the original phenol hydrogens are replaced by alkyl radicals they are not prone to oxidation in like manner as the phenols, hence, presumably do not take part in pigment formation.

Monohydroxy thymoquinone[6]) is believed to occur in *Monarda fistulosa, Monarda citriodora*, and perhaps in other species of *Monarda.*

Dihydroxy thymoquinone[7]) has been isolated from the volatile oils of *Monarda fistulosa* and *Monarda citriodora.* Its presence has been indicated in *Monarda didyma.*

The chemical relationship of the thymoquinones to some of the other constituents of the *Monardas* is very close and is worthy of notice here. From the volatile oils of the several species of *Monarda* so far examined, have been isolated both of the monohydroxy phenols, thymol and carvacrol, and probably cymene[8]) the hydrocarbon underlying not only these phenols but hydrothymoquinone as well.

The relation of the pigment substances to each other and to the volatile constituents of the Monardas, also the role which some of the non-colored volatile and non-volatile substances

[2] C. r., 139, 927.
[3] Schimmel, Gesch. Ber. 1906, Apr. p. 28.
[4] Gildemeister—The Volatile Oils, p. 479.
[5] Personal communication from Prof. E. R. Miller, Laboratory of Plant Chemistry, University of Wisconsin.
[6] Bulletin of the University of Wisconsin No. 448, p. 31–34.
[7] Bulletin of the University of Wisconsin No. 448, p. 31–34.
[8] Ph. Rund., 13, p. 207; Ph. Rev., 14, p. 223. (The writer has not succeeded in identifying cymene in her study of the hydrocarbons in the oil of M. punctata.)

play in the formation of the pigments, can best be illustrated by a series of graphical formulas given on the accompanying chart.

From this chart it becomes apparent that here we have to deal with white (or colorless), yellow, orange, and red substances, all of which are very closely related to each other. Moreover, the thymoquinone, monohydroxythymoquinone and dihydroxythymoquinone, have the capacity of adding monatomic phenols, thus yielding highly colored phenoquinones; also diatomic phenols thus yielding the equally highly colored quinhydrones.

Thymoquinhydrone has actually been isolated from the corollas of Monarda fistulosa while the formation of phenoquinones and quinhydrones of mono- and dihydroxythymoquinone has been considered as a probable explanation of the complexity of the mixture of crystalline pigment originally referred to as "alizarin-like[9])." The following table illustrates the phenoquinone and quinhydrone pigments that can result from the addition of the phenols to the quinones thus far observed in the Monardas.

---

[9] Ph. Rev., 19, p. 244; Mid. Drug., Ph. Rev., 44, p. 342; Bulletin of the Univ. of Wis., No. 448, p. 22.

Cymene

Carvacrol

Thymol

Hydrothymoquinone

Thymoquinone

α-Monohydroxythymequinone

β-Monohydroxythymequinone

Dihydroxythymoquinone

Quinones	*Phenoquinones*	*Quinhydrones*
Thymoquinone	1.) With two molecules of thymol. 2.) With two molecules of carvacrol. 3.) With one molecule each of thymol & carvacrol. 4.) With two molecules of α-monohydroxythymoquinone. 5.) With two molecules of β-monohydroxythymoquinone 6.) With one molecule each of α- & β-monohydroxythymoquinone. 7.) With one molecule each of α-monohydroxythymoquinone and thymol. 8.) With one molecule each of α-monohydroxythymoquinone and carvacrol. 9.) With one molecule each of β-monohydroxythymoquinone and thymol. 10.) With one molecule each of β-monohydroxythymoquinone and carvacrol.	1.) With hydrothymoquinone. 2.) With dihydroxythymoquinone.

Quinones	*Phenoquinones*	*Quinhydrones*
		1.) With hydrothymoquinone. 2.) With dihydroxythymoquinone.
α-Hydroxythymoquinone.	1.) With two molecules of thymol. 2.) With two molecules of carvacrol. 3.) With one molecule each of thymol and carvacrol. 4.) With two molecules of α-monohydroxythymoquinone. 5.) With two molecules of β-monohydroxythymoquinone 6.) With one molecule each of α- and β-monohydroxythymoquinone. 7.) With one molecule each of α-monohydroxythymoquinone and thymol. 8.) With one molecule each of β-monehydroxythymoquinone and carvacrol. 9.) With one molecule each of β-monohydroxythymoquinone and thymol. 10.) With one molecule each of β-mono-hydroxythymoquinone and carvacrol.	

Quinones	*Phenoquinones*	*Quinhydrones*
		1.) With hydrothymoquinone. 2.) With dihydroxythymoquinone.
	1.) With two molecules of thymol.	
	1.) With two molecules of carvacrol.	
	3.) With one molecule each of thymol and carvacrol.	
β-Hydroxythymoquinone.	4.) With two molecules of α-monohydroxythymoquinone.	
	5.) With two molecules of β-monohydroxythymoquinone.	
	6.) With one molecule each of α- and β-monohydroxythymoquinone.	
	7.) With one molecule each of α-monohydroxythymoquinone and thymol.	
	8.) With one molecule each of α-monohydroxythymoquinone and carvacrol.	
	9.) With one molecule each of β-monohydroxythymoquinone and thymol.	
	10.) With one molecule each of β-monohydroxythymoquinone and carvacrol.	

Quinones	*Phenoquinones*	*Quinhydrones*
		1.) With hydrothymoquinone.
		2.) With dihydroxythymoquinone.
	1.) With two molecules of thymol.	
	2.) With two molecules of carvacrol.	
	3.) With one molecule each of thymol and carvacrol.	
Dihydroxythymoquinone.	4.) With two molecules of α-monohydroxythymoquinone.	
	5.) With two molecules of β-monohydroxythymoquinone.	
	6.) With one molecule each of α- and β-monohydroxythymoquinone.	
	7.) One molecule each of α-monohydroxythymoquinone and thymol.	
	8.) With one molecule each of β-monohydroxythymoquinone and thymol.	
	9.) With one molecule each of α-monohydroxythymoquinone and carvacrol.	
	10.) With one molecule each of β-monohydroxythymoquinone and carvacrol.	

Taking into consideration only those compounds that have been isolated, (hydrothymoquinone, thymoquinone, and dihydroxythymoquinone) or whose presence has been indicated (monohydroxythymoquinone) in the Monardas thus far, the number of possible pigments becomes truly bewildering. A consideration of these possibilities of easily decomposable phenoquinones and quinhydrones readily explains why a crystalline pigment, seemingly a chemical unit, upon recrystallization from such a solvent as ether yields several kinds of crystals of different shades of red and purple. To attempt the isolation of a number of these pigments would seem a thankless task. Indeed, after they had been isolated the question might pertinently be asked whether the combination as isolated existed as such in the plant or whether it had been formed because of a change of solvents.

However, the subject of the pigmentation of the Monardas is not solved even after the numerous combinations of phenoquinones and quinhydrones have been worked out. Most of these pigments are phenolic in character and hence can combine with metallic constituents, ammonia and organic nitrogen bases of the plants giving rise to different shades of the original pigment.

This is shown by the varying shades of color produced by treating solutions of these phenols with solutions of basic metallic compounds, etc. However, nothing definite is known of the particular kind of metallic and other derivatives which may be found in the various parts of the several Monarda species.

Another possible influence of basic inorganic material remains to be referred to, viz: the stimulating influence some of them, such as potassium hydroxide and calcium hydroxide, exert on oxidizing reactions, e. g. the oxidation of thymoquinone. That even very dilute basic solutions exert such an influence has been shown by the action of lime water upon aqueous thymoquinhydrone solution. It has further been demonstrated by Schaer[10] and others that traces of basic substances, organic as well as inorganic, stimulate the action of oxidases.

Assuming that much of the pigmentation of plants containing quinones or hydroquinones is due to the formation of quinhydrones or phenoquinones, the intense coloration of the

[10] From a reprint from the Pharm. Inst. Strassburg, 1902.

lower surfaces of the leaves, and often of the entire shoots of *Monarda fistulosa,* and the general reddish appearance of the young plants of *Monarda punctata* in spring can readily be accounted for by the greater oxidase content of the vigorous young tissue and the consequent greater chemical activity.[1] A similar phenomenon in the young plants or shoots after the fall rains may be explained in the same way.

On the other hand, the fall coloration of arbutin containing foliage may be explained by assuming that as the synthetic life processes of the plant grow sluggish, the reserve carbohydrates stored away in the glucoside are rendered available as food material by hydrolysis. This latter process would set free the hydroquinone as well as the sugar. The former (chromogen) in turn would be oxidized to pigment. If this line of reasoning may be applied to the madrones as well as to the other species of arbutus, the brilliant coloration of both the enormous leaf buds in spring and of the leaves and the freshly peeled trunk in autumn may be accounted for.

It has been pointed out above that the diethers of the hydrothymoquinone, being deprived of their phenolic hydrogen are no longer prone to oxidation, hence to quinhydrone pigment formation. It is, therefore, not surprising that plants characterized by the presence of the dimethyl ether of hydrothymoquinone are not conspicuously colored. The only pigmentation of the Eupatorium species which could be attributed to quinhydrone formation is the occasional purplish coloration of the stems.

This purplish stem coloration though not conspicuous deserves special notice since most of the plants considered in this chapter are remarkable at some period of their development, generally late in the season, for conspicuously colored stems, the members of the Ericaceae, trailing arbutus, wintergreen, manzinitas, and mandrones for red or red brown stems, the characteristic color of benzo quinhydrone, while the stems of the Monardas are often conspicuously purple, the color of thymoquinhydrone.

Many investigators have inferred that ferments—hydrolases, oxidases, and reductases—play an important role in pigment

---

[1] The oxidase content of the Monardas has been studied both quantitatively and qualitatively by F. Rabak, Ph. Rev., 22, p. 190; Swingle, Ph Rev., 22, p. 193; Wakeman, Ph. Rev., 26, p. 314.

formation. No where would this part seem more conspicuous than in the formation of quinhydrone and pheno-quinone pigments. Indeed one of the first questions which arises in the biochemical study of any such series of related compounds as the cymene, thymol, carvacrol, hydrothymoquinone, monohydroxy thymoquinone and dihydroxy thymoquinone series in the Monarda species is which of these complex cyclic substances was first formed from the simple chain products of photo synthesis? Being accustomed for purposes of classification to look upon the hydrocarbons as basal compounds and to consider all other compounds as being derived from the hydrocarbons, it is easy to regard such a series as being formed in this order. However, it is highly improbable that the plant works in this way. An oxidase which oxidises hydrothymoquinone to thymoquinone exists in several species of Monarda, but up to the present time no oxygen conveyer has been found which oxidizes thymol or carvacrol to hydrothymoquinone, all attempts in this direction having been attended with negative results, or in the case of thymol, sometimes, with the formation of dithymol. It is not at all improbable that the monatomic phenols and the hydrocarbons are reduction products, possibly by products of autoxidation. The large amounts, however, in which the monatomic phenols are found in comparison with the amounts of thymoquinone and its oxidation products present does not encourage this assumption.

Of almost equal interest with the thymoquinone series of compounds in the Monarda species are the less complete, possibly because less closely investigated, series of carvacrol, hydrothymoquinone, and thymoquinone in *Callistris quadrivalvis* (*Thuja articulata*) and the cymene, hydrothymoquinone series of *Foeniculum vulgare*. Another similar example which should be mentioned here is *Thymus vulgaris*. The oil of thyme is known to contain cymene, thymol, and sometimes carvacrol. Other members of the series, if not present in the original oil, are possibly produced upon standing, since oil of thyme, quite colorless when freshly distilled, often, upon standing, takes on a red color quite similar to the color of the oil from *Monarda fistulosa* from which dihydroxythymoquinone has been separated.

The fact that so frequently the pigment forming substance does not occur alone but is associated with other closely related, colored or non colored, compounds is of much biochemical significance as will be pointed out in succeeding chapters.

Pigments referable to hydrocarbons of the degree of saturation $C_n\ H_{2n-6}$.

There exist in plants several compounds referable to hydrocarbons falling under this degree of saturation, being substitution products of benzene, toluene and cymene, which though colorless in themselves are readily oxidized to pigments. Moreover, being hydroquinones, they are capable of forming highly colored phenoquinones and quinhydrones by addition with their oxidation products the quinones. These compounds occur in a large number of plants either in the free state, as alkyl ethers, or in sugar ether combination as glucosides and they may be looked upon as pigment forming substances, commonly designated chromogens in pigment literature.

While no attempt is being made here at a discussion of the pigments of non-flowering plants it is interesting to note that there exist in several species of lichens pigments and pigment forming substances referrable to the hydrocarbons toluene, o-xylene, p-xylene and trimethyl 1, 2, 4 benzene.

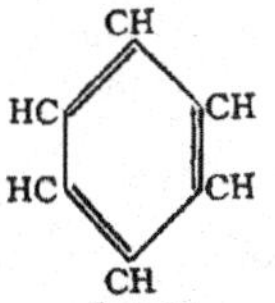

CH, HC, CH, HC, CH, CH

Benzene

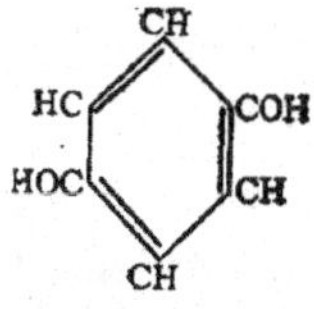

CH, HC, COH, HOC, CH, CH

Hydroquinone

The only known pigment, or pigment forming substance, referable to benzene as the underlying hydrocarbon is the ordinary hydroquinone, or hydrobenzoquinone. The occurrence of hydroquinone as the glucoside arbutin in several species of *Ericaceae* and the possibility of its forming the corresponding quinone and quinhydrone through oxidation thus furnishing an explanation for the pigmentation of several species has been referred to under benzoquinone.

Arbutin occurs in *Ledum palustre*[1]; *Rhododendron maxi-*

[1] Am. Jr. Ph., 46, p. 314.

mum,[2]) *Kalmia latifolia*,[3]) *Kalmia angustifolia*,[4]) *Gaultheria procumbens*,[5]) *Arctostaphylos Uva Uris*,[6]) *Arctostaphylos glauca*,[7]) *Vaccinium Myrtillus*,[8]) *Vaccinium vitis*,[9]) *Vaccinium macrocarpum*,[10]) *Vaccinium arctostaphylos*,[11]) *Calluna vulgaris*,[12]) *Erica herbacea*,[13]) *Pinus communis*,[14]) *Protea millifera*,[15]) *Chimaphila umbellata*,[16]) *Chimaphila maculata*,[17]) and *Pirola uniflora*.[18])

In addition to the above, the mono-ethyl ether of hydroquinone has been found in the oil of star anise, *Illicium verum*.[19]) Furthermore it has been pointed out that the pentatomic alcohol of hexahydrobenzene, quercite,[20]) may lose three of its hydroxy groups in the form of water and form hydroquinone as indicated by the following formula:

$$C_6H_7\ (OH)_5 \xrightarrow{-3H_2O} C_6H_4\ (OH)_2$$

Pigments referable to toluene

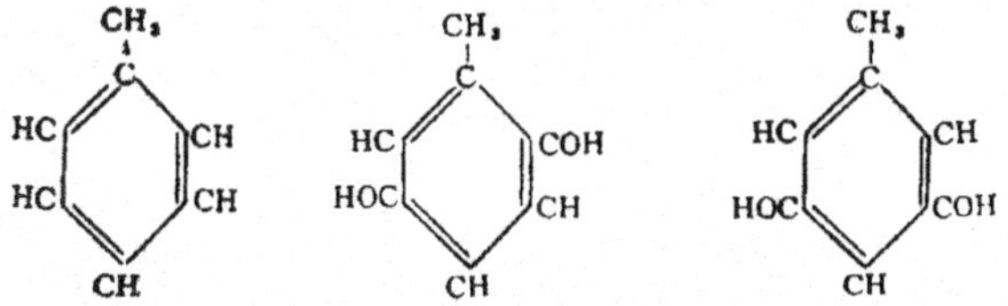

CH_3–C; HC, CH; HC, CH; CH	CH_3–C; HC, COH; HOC, CH; CH	CH_3–C; HC, CH; HOC, COH; CH
Toluene	**Hydrotoluquinone** or **Methyl hydrobenzoquinone** or **Methyl-hydroquinone**	**Orcinol**

[2] Wehmer, Die Pflanzenstoffe, p. 570.
[3] Am. J. Ph., 47, p. 5.
[4] Am. J. Ph., 58, p. 417.
[5] Am. Jr. Ph., 46, p. 314.
[6] Arch. Pharm., 227, p. 164; Am. Jr. Ph., 46, p. 314.
[7] Am. Jr. Ph., 46, p. 314.
[8] Monatsh f. Chem., 30, p. 77.
[9] Arch. exper. Path., u. Pharm., 50, 46.
[10] Chem. News, 52, 78.
[11] Apoth. Ztg., 16, 694.
[12] Am. Jr. Ph., 46, 314.
[13] S. Ber. Wien. Acad., 9, 308.
[14] Jr. Pharm. Chim. (7) 2, 248.
[15] B. 29, R. P. 416.
[16] An. Chim., 129, 203.
[17] Am. Jr. Ph., 46, 314.
[18] Am. Jr. Ph., 11, 549.
[19] Schimmel & Co., Oct., 1895, p. 6.
[20] Plant Pigments, p. 11.

Methyl hydroquinone occurs as the glucoside methyl arbutin in several species of *Ericaceae.*[21]) It is also known to exist in several species of *Pirola*[22]) and in *Pirus communis.*[23])

Orcinol an isomer of methyl hydroquinone and referable to toluene is found in many lichens of the varieties *Rocella* and *Lecenora.* Orcinol[24]) when allowed to stand exposed to air and ammonia forms orcein $C_7H_7NO_3$, the principal constituent of the coloring matter archil, called also persio, cudbear and nurpur. Azolithmin[25]) $C_7H_7NO_4$, the coloring principle of litmus and an oxidation product of orcein, is also produced from these orcinol containing lichens by the action of ammonia and potassium carbonate.

Pigments referable to trimethyl 1, 2, 4 benzene.

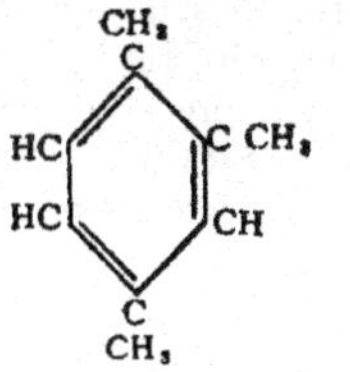

Trimethyl 1, 2, 4, benzene

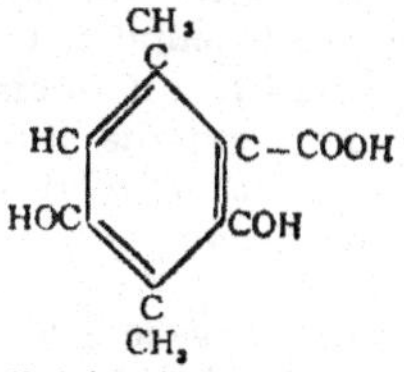

Methyl orsellinic acid

In one variety of *Rocella* there occurs a homologue of erythrin known as betaerythrin.[26]) This upon hydrolysis yields not orcinol but beta orcinol, or methyl orcinol, p-xylol orcinol. At least one molecule of the simple acids combined to form the betaerythrin is therefore probably methyl orsellinic acid, referable to trimethyl 1, 2, 4 benzene.

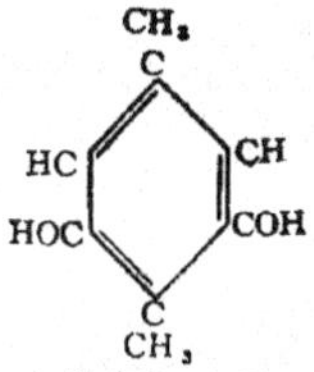

Methyl orcinol

[21] Ann., 206, 159; Ann., 177, 934.
[22] Am. J. Ph., 11, p. 549.
[23] Jr. Pharm. Chim., (7) 2, 248; C. r., 151. p. 444.
[24] Ann., 41, p. 157; 54, p. 261; 59, p. 72; Jr. Prakt. Chem., 44, p. 18.
[25] Ann., 39, p. 25; Czapek, Biochemie der Pflanzen, p. 508.
[26] Czapek, Biochemie der Pflanzen, p. 507.

Pigments referable to o-xylene

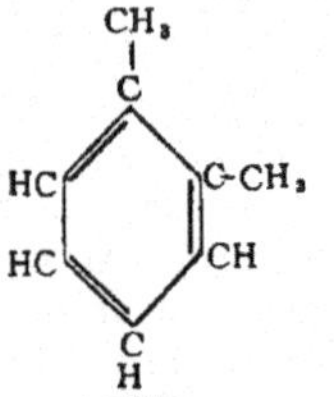

o-xylene

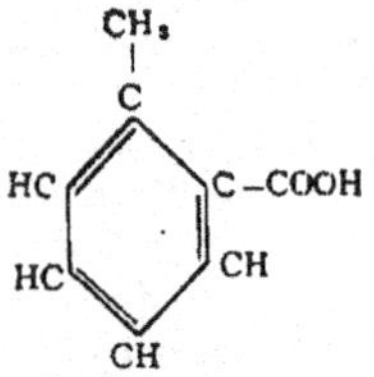

Orsellinic acid

Lecanoric acid,[27]) another pigment forming substance from some varieties of *Roccella, Lecanora,* and *Variolaria,* is probably a condensation product of two molecules of orsellinic acid, referable to o-xylene, dimethyl 1, 2, benzene.

Lecanoric acid crystallizes in colorless crystals. With alkalies it gives a beautiful rose like color, with calcium chloride, a blood red color. It occurs combined with erythrite as the ester, lecanoryl erythrite, also known as erythrin.

The constitution of other similar pigments found in these lichens is not known.

Pigments referable to cymene

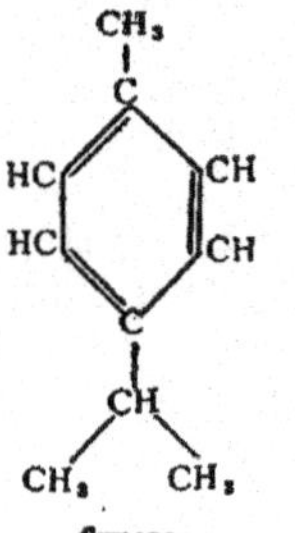

Cymene

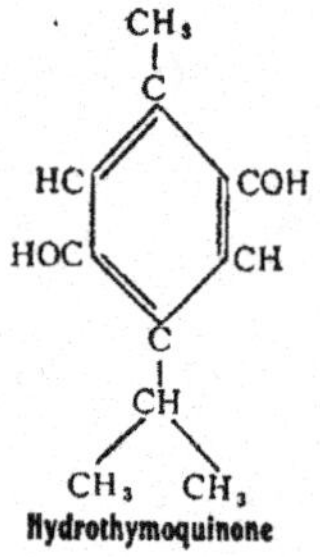

Hydrothymoquinone

Hydrothymoquinone has already been discussed in connection with thymoquinone in the preceding chapter. It occurs

[27] Ann., 295, p. 278; 41, p. 157; 54, p. 261; 61, p. 72; Jr. Prakt. Chim. 44, p. 18; Czapek, Biochemie der Pflanzen, p. 507.

along with thymoquinone in several species of ***Monarda***, also in ***Thuja articulata***. Its occurrence as dimethyl ether[28]) in the oils of ***Eupatorium triplinerve*** and ***Eupatorium capillifolium***, as well as in the oil from ***Arnica Montana*** has also been noted.

PIGMENTS REFERABLE TO HYDROCARBONS OF THE FORMULA OF SATURATION $C_n H_{2n-8}$.

The only plant pigments of known constitution referable to hydrocarbons falling under this degree of saturation are substitution products of phenyl ethene and phenyl propene, propenyl benzene.

Pigments referable to phenyl ethene.

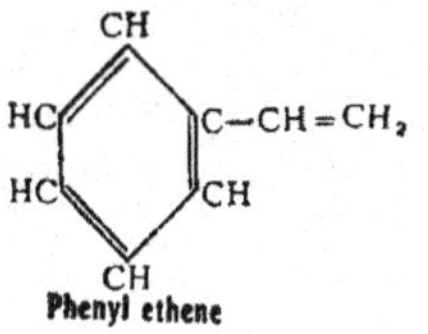

Phenyl ethene

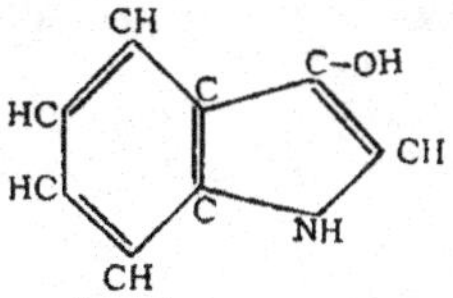

Indoxyl

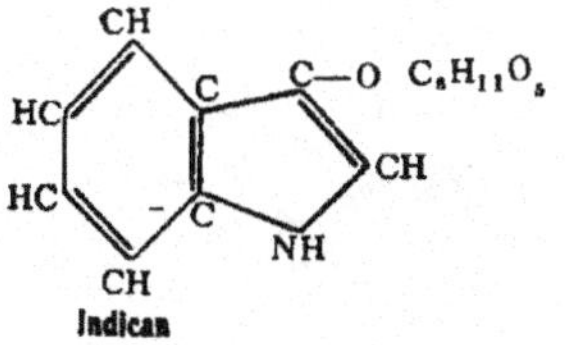

Indican

Indican occurs in indigo bearing plants almost exclusively in the form of the glucoside indican,* a sugar ether of indoxyl, referable to phenyl ethene. Upon treatment of the herb, or the indigo producing part thereof, with water the glucoside is extracted. This is hydrolized by an enzyme present in the plant. By contact with the air the indoxyl thus produced is oxidized to indigotin.

[28] See references to preceding chapter.

[29] Ann. Chem., 170, p. 345.

*For references to indican and indoxl see Indigotin, formula of saturation CnH2n-16.

Pigments referable to allyl benzene

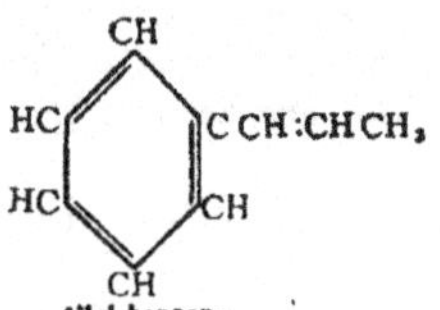

Allyl benzene

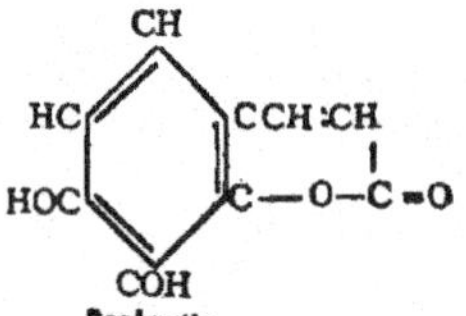

Daphnetin

As will be seen from the structural formula, daphnetin may be looked upon as a dihydroxy cumarin, or as a product of the inner condensation, a lactone, of tri-hydroxy cinnamic acid. Since the occurrence of daphentin in the plant is so frequently accompanied by that of cumarin, umbelliferone and other cinnamic acid derivatives, the importance of recognizing this relationship cannot be over estimated.

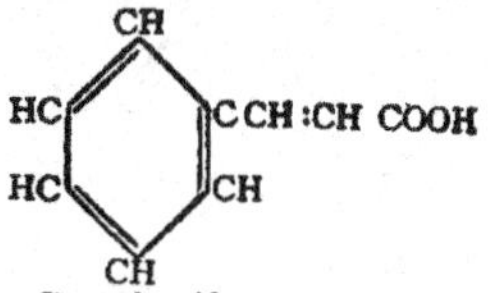

Cinnamic acid

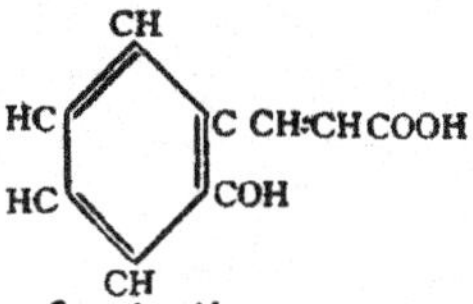

Cumaric acid

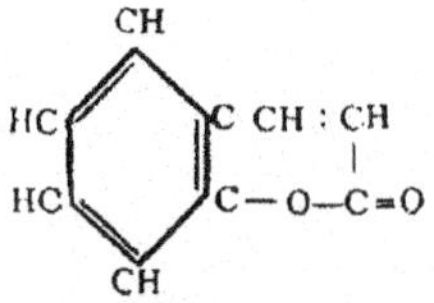

Cumarin

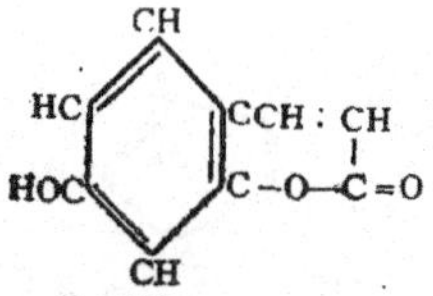

Umbelliferone

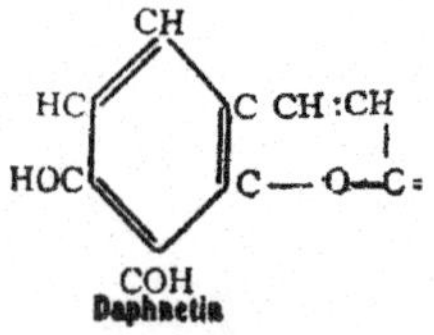

Daphnetin

Daphnetin which is yellow in color, occurs in the yellow flowers of sweet clover, *Mililotus officinalis*.[1].) together with cumarin, cumaric acid, and hydro cumaric[2]) acid. The frequency of the occurrence of these and related compounds in this and other members of the *Leguminosae* will be taken up in the consideration of pigmentation in that family.

Daphnetin, having two phenol hydrogens, is capable of forming metallic derivatives which may influence the color of the pigmented parts. With potassium it forms the socalled "semi-

[1] Berg. Jahresb., 14, 31¹.
[2] Richter, II, p. 280.

mono potassium salt" $C_{18}H_{11}O_8K$ and the mono potassium salt $C_9H_5O_4K$. The former crystallizes in bright yellow and the latter in red crystals. To wools mordanted with chromium, aluminum, tin and iron it imparts various shades of olive and yellow.

Daphnetin occurs as the glucoside daphnin, in the bark and flowers of *Daphne mezerum*[3]) and in the leaves, bark and flowers of *Daphne alpina.*[4]) In these plants, however, the odoriferous principle is not cumarin but umbelliferone, a 4-hydroxy cumarin.

Daphnin, or a glucoside similar to daphnin has, furthermore, been reported in *Panicum italicum*[5]) (Italian millet.)

Closely related to daphnetin are aesculetin, scopoletin, and fraxetin, substances which though not colored themselves form beautifully fluorescent solutions. Moreover, at least some of their metallic derivatives, in which form they would be likely to occur in plants, are colored.

Aesculetin is isomeric with daphnetin, being a 4, 5-dihydroxy cumarin. It forms a bright yellow potassium compound very similar to the corresponding daphnetin derivative. Its solutions show a beautiful blue fluorescence. Aesculetin occurs as the glucoside aesculin in *Aesculus hippocastanum,*[6]) the horse chestnut, and in *Gelsemium sempervirens.*[7]) In the free state, it is found in *Euphorbia lathyris.*[8])

Scopoletin, a methyl ether of aesculetin occurs as the glucoside scopolin in *Gelsemium sempervirens,*[10]) and in several species of *Solanaceae, Atropa belladonna,*[11]) *Scopola japonica,*[12]) *Mandragora autumnalis,*[13]) and *Fabiana imbricata.*[14]) Scopoletin gives a blue fluorescence in solutions. Many of its metallic derivatives are colored.

Fraxetin, another beautiful fluorescent substance is a derivative of tetra hydroxy cinnamic acid. It may be considered as a

---

[3] Ann., 84, 173.
[4] Zwenger's Ann., 115, 1.
[5] Am. Chem. Jr., 20, 86.
[6] Arch. Pharm., 38, 330.
[7] Ber., 9, 1182.
[8] Ber., 23, 3347.
[9] Czapek—Biochemie der Pflanzen, p. 563.
[10] Am. Jr. Ph., 42, p. 1; 54, p. 337; Arch. Pharm., 236, p. 329.
[11] Arch. Pharm. 228, p. 438, 440.
[12] Same as 11.
[13] Jr. Prakt. Chem., 172, p. 274.
[14] Arch. Pharm., 237, p. 1.

methyl ether of hydroxy daphnetin or aesculetin, or as a methyl ether of trihydroxy cumarin.

Fraxetin occurs along with aesculetin as the glucoside fraxin in the horse chestnut.[15]) It occurs as the glucoside fraxin in *Fraxinus excelsior*,[16]) *Fraxinus ornus*,[17]) also both in the free state and as glucoside in *Fraxinus americana*.[18])

Fraxetin gives a blue fluorescence in solutions. Many of its metallic derivatives are colored. The position of the methoxy group in fraxetin is not known.

PIGMENTS REFERABLE TO HYDROCARBONS OF THE FORMULA OF SATURATION C_nH_{2n-10}.

Under this formula of saturation one pigment of known constitution, juglone, referable to dihydro naphthalene, and two others probably derivatives of methyl dihydro naphthalene have been isolated. All three of these compounds are hydroxy naphthaquinones, possessing both phenol and quinone properties and capable of forming phenoquinones and quinhydrones with themselves and with the corresponding hydroquinones. In addition to these naphthaquinone pigments one, referable to di-dihydro phenyl ethane has been isolated.

Pigments referable to dihydro naphthalene.

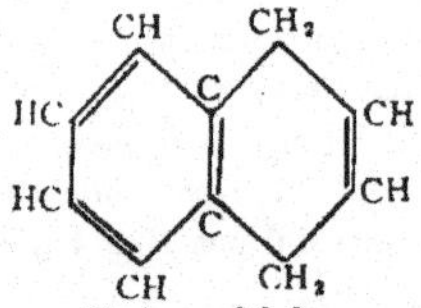

dihydro naphthalene

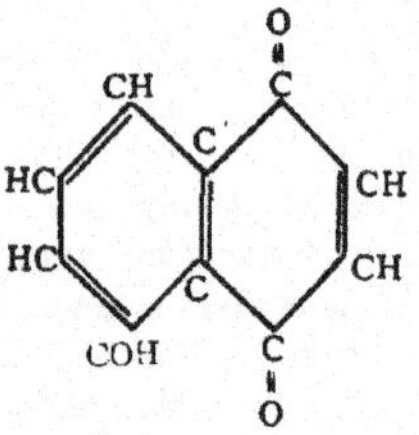

Juglone

Juglone, a hydroxy derivative of naphtha quinone, is found in all the green parts of the walnut tree, *Juglans regia*,[1]) and especially in the green shells of the nuts. Associated with it

---

[15] Pogg. Ann., 107, p. 331.
[16] Pogg. Ann., 98, p. 637.
[17] Pogg. Ann., 98, p. 637; C. r. 51, p. 31.
[18] Am. Jr. Ph., 54. 282: 54. 99.
[1] C. r., 141, p. 838; Ber. Repert., 5, p. 106; 7, p. 1; Ber., 10, p. 1542.

in the twigs, bark, leaves and shell of the unripe fruit, but not in the shells of ripe nuts, α and β-hydrojuglones, trihydroxy naphthalenes, are also found. These colorless hydrojuglones, during the ripening of the nuts, are undoubtedly oxidized to the yellowish red juglone. Indeed the oxidation may well be carried farther, for juglone is readily oxidized by exposure to the air into hydroxy juglones which are still darker in color. There is no record, however, of the hydroxy juglones having been isolated from the walnut material. Juglone is also found in the green shells of the nuts and the bark of the twigs of *Juglans nigra*, the black walnut, *Juglans cinerea*,[2]) the butternut; in the leaves of *Carya olivaeformis*,[2]) the pecan; and in the bark of the twigs of *Pterocarya caucasia*.[2])

The possibilities for combination between juglone and the hydrojuglones must not be overlooked in considering the dark colored pigments in the walnut shells. Not only is there the possibility of juglone combining with each α and β-hydrojuglone to form the corresponding quinhydrones; but the additional possibilities of its forming phenoquinones with itself, through the addition of its phenol group to a carbonyl group, and also of forming phenoquinones with the hydro juglones. If juglone be oxidized in the plant to hydroxy juglones the possibilities for pheno quinone and quinhydrone formation become fully as great as with the thymoquinones in the *Monarda* species.

Pigments referable to a methyl dihydro naphthalene

$C_{10}H_9CH_3$	$C_{10}H_5O_2CH_3$
Methyldihydro-Naphthalene	Methyldihydro-Naphthaquinone
$C_{10}H_3O_2(OH)_2CH_3$	$C_{10}H_2(OH)_3O_2CH_3$
Dihydroxy-methyl Naphthaquinone	Trihydroxy-methyl Naphthaquinone

Two pigments, one orange red, crystallizing in needles, and the other red, crystallizing in plates, have been isolated from the root tubers of *Drosera Whittakeri*. The former is apparently dihydroxy methyl naphthaquinone and the latter trihydroxy methyl naphthaquinone.

Pigmentation in *Drosera Whittakeri* seems to be confined to

[2] C. r., 141, p. 838.

the tubers. According to Rennie[1]) who has made a study of these pigments, each plant is provided with one tuber attached to a stem at a depth of 3 to 4 inches. The tubers vary from ¼ to ¾ of an inch in diameter. Each consists of an inner solid but soft nucleus, full of a reddish sap, and an outer series of thin, more or less dry, layers of an almost black material. Between the layers is to be found, in small quantities, a brilliant red coloring matter, apparently most plentiful in the older tubers. The flowers of the species are white, resembling those of the white oxalis. The red pigment gives a violet, the orange red a deep red solution with ammonia and alkalies.

This remarkable form of pigmentation is doubly interesting when considered from the view point of the quinhydrone hypothesis. Both of the substances are quinones, and both have in addition phenol groups. The presence of the corresponding hydroquinones has not been indicated, though both substances may be reduced to hydroquinones. Whether the black outer layers owe their color to phenoquinones, quinhydrones or higher oxidation products of the known pigments does not become apparent from Rennie's investigations, though the red crystals between the dark layers are apparently the trihydroxy compound.

Pigments referable to di-dihydrophenyl-ethane.

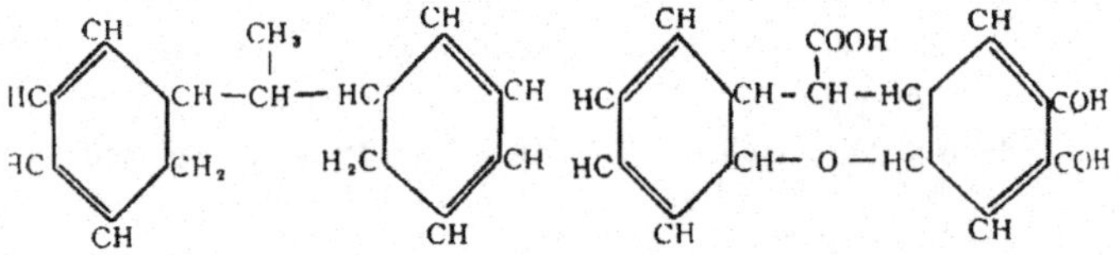

Di-dihydro phenyl ethane

Phoeniceine

Phoeniceine[1].) occurs as the colorless leuco-compound phoenin in the heart of wood of *Copaifera bracteata*, the "purpurholz" "amaranth wood" or "blue ebony" of South America, comprising about two per cent of the wood. Phoenin, C_{14} H_{16} O_7, upon treatment with mineral acids gives up one

[1] Chem. News, 55, p. 115; Jr. Chem. Soc., 51, p. 371; 63, p. 1083.

[1] Kleerekoper, E. Neederl. Tijdschr. Pharm., 13, p. 245; 284, 303. (Chem. Centralbl. 72, II, p. 858, 1085).

molecule of water forming quantitatively the red phoeniceine $C_{14} H_{14} O_6$. This reaction also takes place quantitatively upon long heating at 100° or heating for one hour at 150°–160°. Upon exposure to the air at ordinary temperature phoenin passes slowly to phoeniceine.

Upon treatment with alkalies phoeniceine turns blue, then violet, and finally brown in color. Its behavior toward alkalies and acids is similar to that of the flavone compounds containing two hydroxy groups in ortho position. Kleerekoper[1]) suggests the formula given above.

Pigments referable to hydrocarbons of the formula of saturation C_nH_{2n-12}.

There exist in plants several pigments and pigment forming substances referable to hydrocarbons of this degree of saturation, all of which are substitution products of four different hydrocarbons, namely, naphthalene, two dihydro naphthalene derivatives with unsaturated side chains, and phenyl-diphenyl methane.

Pigments referable to Naphthalene.

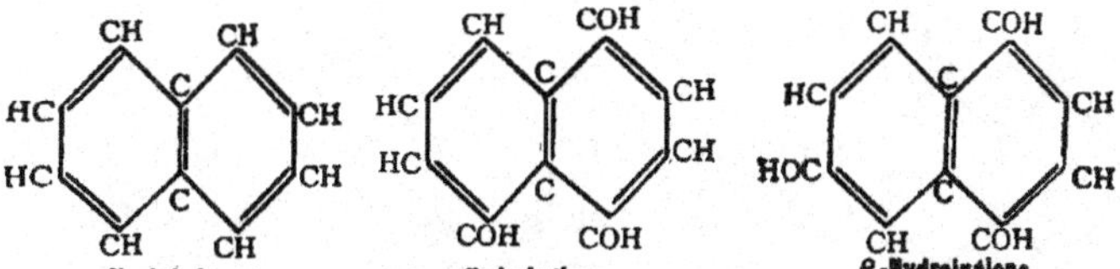

Naphthalene α Hydrojuglone β-Hydrojuglone

Both of the hydro juglones exist, along with juglone, in all the green parts of the walnut tree, *Juglans regia.*[1]) Upon oxidation α hydrojuglone yields juglone. A discussion of the various quinhydrones and phenoquinones which may be formed by combination of the two hydrojuglones with juglone, also with possible higher oxidation products of juglone, has been given under juglone.

[1] Ber., 10, p. 1544; 17, p. 2411; 18, p. 204; 18, p. 474; 18, p. 2567.
[2] Jr. Chem. Soc., 69, p. 1355.

Pigments referable to methyl 2, butylene 2, dihydro naphthalene.

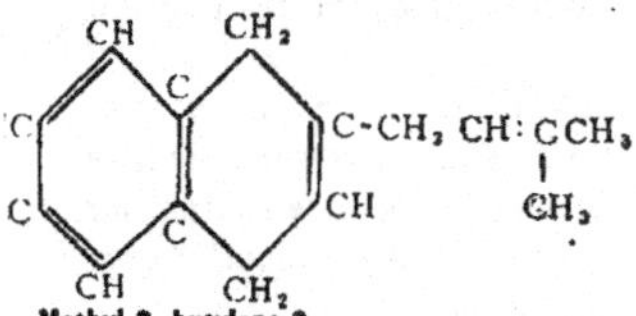

Methyl 2, butylene 2 dihydro naphthalene

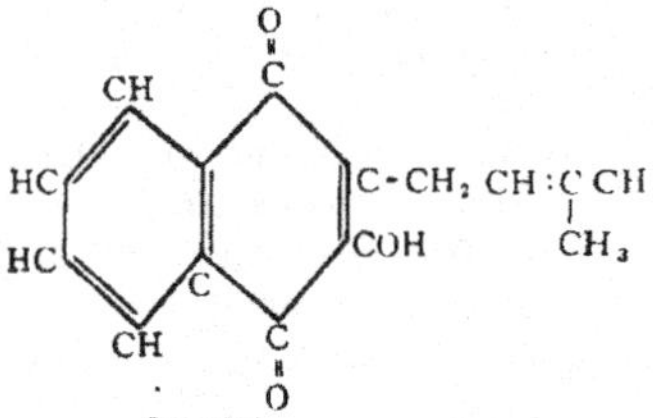

Lapachol

A hydroxy amylene naphthaquinone, lapachol, yellow in color, has been found in the lapacho[3]) wood, obtained from several species of South American *Bignoniaceae,* in the green heart of Surinam[4]) and in Bethabarra wood.[5])

Upon reduction with sodium, lapachol yields an unstable hydrolapachol. The metallic derivatives of lapachol are of various shades of red and orange red.

Pigments referable to methyl 2, butylene 3, dihydro naphthalene.

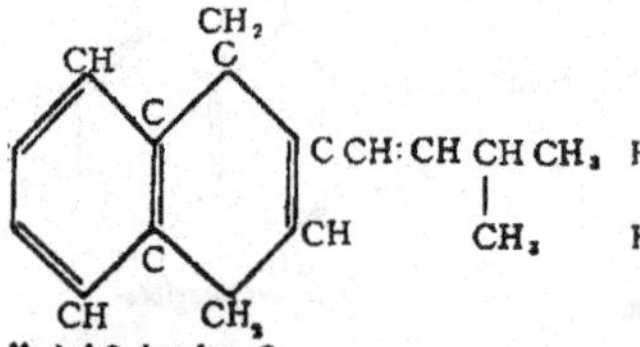

Methyl 2, butylene 3 dihydro naphthalene

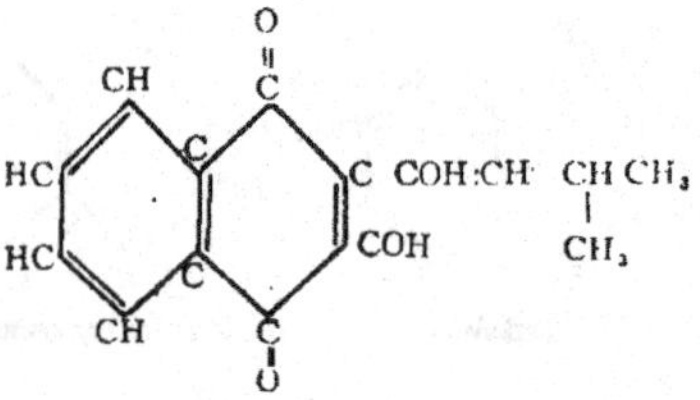

Lomatiol

A yellow compound, lomatiol,[6]) hydroxy lapachol or oxyisolapachol, has been isolated from the seeds of *Lomatia ilicifolia* and *Lomatia longifolia.*

The metallic derivatives of lomatiol are red, orange or brown in color.

---

[3] Jahresb. u. d. Fortsch. d. Chem., (1858) p. 264.
[4] Ztsch. f. Chem., (1867) p. 92.
[5] Am. Chem., Jr., 11, p. 267.
[6] Jr. Chem. Soc., 67, 784.

Pigments referable to phenyl-dihydro phenyl methane.

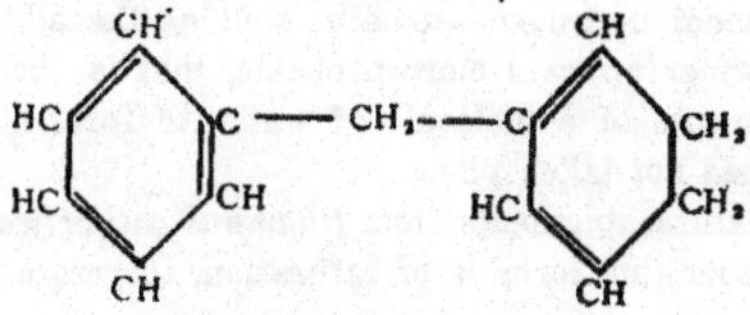

Phenyl-dihydro phenyl-methane

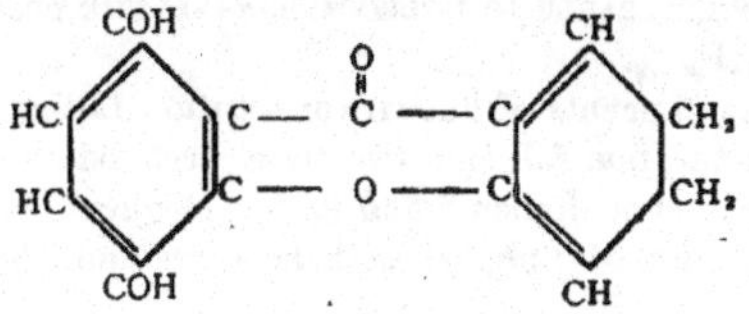

Rhamnocitrin

A group of yellow pigments, some of them supposedly derivatives of the above named hydrocarbon, has been isolated from the berries of *Rhamnus cathartica.*[7]) These pigments are rhamnocitrin, β-rhamnocitrin, rhamnochrisin, rhamnolutin and rhamnonigrin. As will be seen from the formula assigned to rhamnocitrin above, these pigments resemble the xanthone derivatives, falling under the degree of saturation C_nH_{2n-14}, more closely than they do the remaining known pigments of this degree of saturation. They are indeed derivatives of a reduced xanthone nucleus.

Rhamnocitrin occurs, probably, in the free state. It crystallizes in golden yellow needles, and it forms metallic derivatives deeper in color than the compound itself.

β-Rhamnocitrin has the same empirical formula as rhamnocitrin which it closely resembles. To mordanted fabrics it imparts a more enduring color than does rhamnocitrin.

Rhamnochrysin, $C_{13}H_{12}O_7$ crystallizes in orange yellow crystals. It is looked upon as an oxidation product of rhamnocitrin. Whether the molecule is of phenyl-dihydro phenyl

[7] Bull. de Pharm., 4, p. 64; Journ. de Chim. Med., 6, p. 193; Journ. de Pharm. et de Chim., 11, p. 666; Arch. de Pharm., 113, p. 63; Arch. d. Pharm., 238, p. 459.

methanone configuration, or contains the "chromone" group does not appear to have been determined. Since it contains two additional hydrogen atoms as well as the additional oxygen the former appears more probable, that is, the elimination of the elements of a molecule of water to form a heterocycle probably has not taken place.

The remaining pigments from *Rhamnus cathartica* plainly do not fall under this formula of saturation, therefore, will not be considered here.

PIGMENTS REFERABLE TO HYDROCARBONS OF THE DEGREE OF SATURATION C_nH_{2n-14}.

All of the pigments of known constitution falling under this degree of saturation fall into two closely related classes.

I. Derivatives of diphenyl and its homologues.

II. Derivatives of diphenyl methane series and "homologous" series.

Not only are the pigments referable to these closely related hydrocarbons but they are all hydroxy or methoxy—derivatives of these hydrocarbons. They occur in the plant either in the free state or as glucosides, and they resemble each other as closely in properties as they do in general structure.

I. Pigments referable to the diphenyl series and homologues.
   1. Pigments referable to ditolyl.
      a. Ellagic acid.

II. Pigments referable to diphenyl methane series and "homologous" series.
   A. Diphenylmethane series.
      1. Pigments referable to diphenyl methane.
         Cotoin.
         Euxanthone.
         Maclurin.
         Kinoin.
         Gentisein.
            Gentisin.
         Datiscetin.
      2. Pigments referable to phenyl-o-ethophenyl-methane.
         Catechin
         Cyanomaclurin.

B. Diphenylethane series.
   1. Pigments referable to diphenyl ethane.
      Genistein.
C. Diphenylpropane series.
   1. Pigments referable to diphenyl propane.
      Phloretin.
      Butin.
      Saponarin and Vitexin.

I. Pigments referable to the diphenyl series of hydrocarbons.

The only member of this series to which a plant pigment is known to be referable is a dimethyl homologue, the ditolyl.

Pigments referable to ditolyl.

Ditolyl

Ellagic acid

Ellagic acid occurs quite widely distributed in plants, usually accompanied by tannins. It is found in the leaves of *Juglans regia*[1] along with gallic acid and juglone; in the leaves of *Quercus pedunculata*,[2] *Quercus infectoria*,[3] *Caspinus betulus*,[4] *Haematoxylon campechianum*,[5] *Caesalpina brevifolia*,[6] *Caesalpinia coriaria*,[3] *Coriaria myrtifolia*,[5] *Quebrachia lorentzii*,[6] *Tamarax gallica*,[7] *Tamarax africana*,[7] *Donabanga moluccana*,[8] *Punica granatum*,[8] *Terminalia chebula*,[9] *Vaccinium vitis ideaea*.[10]

Ellagic acid forms small yellowish crystals. It dissolves in concentrated sulphuric acid with a citron yellow color. From

[1] C. r., 141, p. 838.
[2] Z. physiol. Chem., 20, p. 511.
[3] Jr. Chem. Soc., 71, p. 1131.
[4] Arch. Pharm., 244, p. 575.
[5] Proc. Chem. Soc., 16, p. 45; Jr. Chem. Soc., 77, p. 426.
[6] Jr. Chem. Soc., 71, p. 1194.
[7] Jr. Chem. Soc., 73, p. 374.
[8] Nederl. Tijdschr. Pharm., 1887, p. 68.
[9] Ber., 42, p. 353.
[10] Chem. News., 52, p. 78; Pharm. Jr., 16, p. 92.

this solution it is precipitated unchanged by water. With potassium hydroxide solution it forms a deep yellow solution which upon exposure to the air goes to a deep reddish yellow. It dyes wools mordanted with chromium a deep olive yellow color.

The formula for ellagic acid given above was suggested by Graebe.[11]. Further work upon the constitution of ellagic acid by Goldschmidt,[12] also by Niernstein,[13] and by Herzig[14] has confirmed Graebe's formula.

II. DERIVATIVES OF THE DIPHENYL METHANE SERIES OF HYDROCARBONS AND "HOMOLOGOUS" SERIES.

By far the greater number of pigments of known constitution falling under the degree of saturation $C_n H_{2n-14}$ are derivatives of the diphenyl methane series and their homologues. Of these diphenyl methane derivatives there are representatives of the diphenyl methane, diphenyl ethane, and diphenyl propane series; but by far the greater number are referable to diphenyl methane.

II. A. 1. *Pigments referable to diphenyl methane.*

All the plant pigments of known constitution referable to diphenyl methane are tri, tetra, penta, or hexa hydroxy substitution products of diphenyl methanone. In some instances it is true methoxy groups are substituted for hydroxy groups, while in others the elements of a molecule of water has been eliminated from the hydroxy groups, thus forming an oxide group. Indeed this latter condensation appears always to have taken place wherever the hydroxy groups are so located that by the elimination of the elements of a molecule of water there can be formed a cycle of six members. Thus some of the pigments of this group are dicyclic while others are tricyclic compounds, the third cycle being heterocyclic in as much as it contains an oxide oxygen. These pigments are all alike in that they form needle like crystals very similar in character, of a pale yellow color, (hence the name xanthone) and of high melting point.

---

[11] Ber., 36, p. 212.
[12] Monatsh. f. Chem., 26, p. 1143.
[13] Ber., 41, p. 1649.
[14] Monatsh. f. Chem., 29, p. 363.

Authorities differ somewhat as to what part or parts of the molecule the coloring properties are due. All seem to agree, however, that it depends largely upon the number of hydroxy groups. A study of the formulae reveals the fact that the property of color appears to depend upon the number of free hydroxy groups, or their oxide equivalent, rather than upon the number originally introduced into the molecule, the changing of the hydroxy groups into methoxy groups appears to diminish both the color of the compound and its dyeing properties. On the other hand the elimination of the elements of a molecule of water from two hydroxy groups to form the xanthone grouping appears to intensify both pigmentation and dyeing quality.

Most writers, in treating of these pigments, distinguish between diphenyl ketone and xanthone derivatives. However, since whether or not a compound falls into the xanthone group depends merely upon the position of hydroxy groups and the consequent elimination of the elements of a molecule of water and the formation of a heterocycle and not upon any more basal constitutional difference, there appears to be no sufficient point to this distinction. Therefore for the sake of simplicity as well as for observing genetic relationships, all of the members of this group, referable to diphenyl methane, will here be regarded as hydroxy derivatives of diphenyl methanone.

II. A. 1. *Pigments referable to diphenyl methane.*

a. Trihydroxides.
  Cotoin.
b. Tetrahydroxides.
  Euxanthone.
    Euxanthonic acid.
c. Penthydroxides.
  Maclurin.
  Kinoin.
d. Hexhydroxides.
  Gentiseine.
    Gentisin.
  Datiscetin.

II. A. 1. a.) *Trihydroxy derivatives of diphenyl methanone.*

Cotoin,—Dihydroxy-2, 6-methoxy-4-diphenyl methanone.

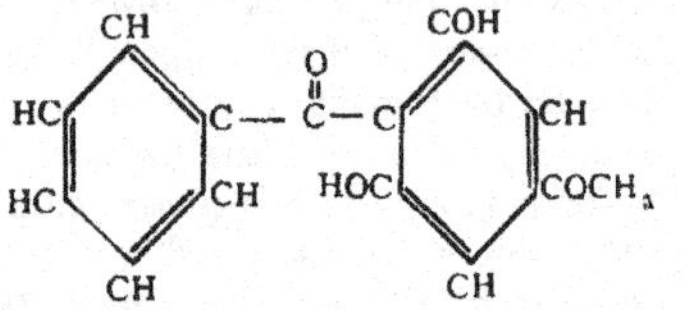

CH COH

O

HC C — C — C CH

HC CH HOC $COCH_3$

CH CH

Cotoin is a trihydroxy derivative of diphenyl ketone, referable to a penthydroxide of the underlying hydrocarbon. It occurs in coto bark[1] and Para coto bark, obtained from Brazil. Cotoin[2] forms colorless or only slightly yellow crystals which melt at 130°. With caustic alkalies it forms a yellow solution. In 1894 Ciamician and Silber[3] partially determined the constitution of cotoin. Pollock,[4] in 1901, completed this by determining the position of the hydroxy groups.

In the bark of *Para coto* cotoin is accompanied by a series of closely related compounds, hydrocotoin, methyl hydrocotoin, protocotoin and methyl protocotoin. These compounds, all of which closely resemble cotoin, were first studied by Jobst and Hesse[5] in 1879. In 1891–1892 Ciamician and Silber[6] made a further investigation of this series of pigments and determined their relation to cotoin and to each other. This relationship is best illustrated by the following series of partly analyzed formulae:

$$C_6H_2\begin{cases} O\,CH_3 \\ O\,H \\ O\,H \\ C\,O\,C_6H_5 \end{cases} \qquad C_6H_2\begin{cases} O\,CH_3 \\ O\,CH_3 \\ O\,H \\ C\,O\,C_6H_5 \end{cases} \qquad C_6H_2\begin{cases} O\,CH_3 \\ O\,CH_3 \\ O\,CH_3 \\ C\,O\,C_6H_5 \end{cases}$$

Cotoin. Hydrocotoin Methyl hydrocotoin

1 Neues. Rept. f. Pharm., 25, p. 23.
2 Ann., 199, p. 17.
3 Ber., 27, p. 1497.
4 Monats., 18, p. 738; 22, p. 996.
5 Ann., 199, p. 17.
6 Ber., 24, p. 299, 2977; 25, p. 1119

$$C_6H_2\begin{cases} O\,CH_3 \\ O\,CH_3 \\ O\,H \\ CO\,C_6\,H_3 \langle {}^{O}_{O} \rangle CH_2 \end{cases} \qquad C_6H_2\begin{cases} O\,CH_3 \\ O\,CH_3 \\ O\,CH_3 \\ CO\,C_6\,H_3 \langle {}^{O}_{O} \rangle CH_2 \end{cases}$$

Protocotoin. Methyl protocotoin.

It will be seen from the above formulae that hydrocotoin is not, as the name implies, a reduced cotoin; but, rather a methyl cotoin, or monohydroxy-dimethoxy-diphenylmethanone. Methyl hydrocotoin is dimethyl cotoin, or trimethoxy-diphenylmethanone. Protocotoin is the methylene ether of a dihydroxy-methylcotoin and methyl protocotoin is a methylene ether of a dihydroxy-dimethylcotoin.

The three compounds possessing free hydroxy groups form colored metallic derivatives. Further studies of cotoin, hydrocotoin and their derivatives have been made by Henrich,[7] Perkin,[8] and others.[9]

II. A. 1. b.) *Tetrahydroxy derivatives of diphenyl methanone.*

Euxanthone,—Dihydroxy-3, 4-diphenylene methanone oxide, or Dihydroxy-3, 4-xanthone.

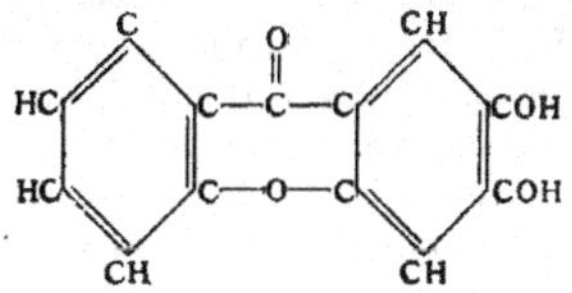

C O CH
HC C—C—C COH
HC C—O—C COH
CH CH

Euxanthone exists partly in the free state and partly in combination with glucoronic acid in "*purree,*" or Indian yellow. Indian yellow is prepared from the urine of cattle fed upon

[7] B., 32, p. 3423.
[8] Jr. Chem. Soc., 71, p. 1194.
[9] Monatsh., 18, p. 142; Ann., 282, p. 191; B., 28, p. 1459; Pharm. Post., 18, p. 179.

mango leaves. Euxanthone was first studied by Stenhouse[1] in 1844 and a little later by Erdman[2] who named both the free euxanthone and the acid compound. In 1889 Graebe[3] synthesized euxanthone and made a study of its structure. The complete structure of the molecule was determined by Kostanecki[4] and Nessler, 1891–1894. As yet euxanthone does not appear to have been isolated directly from the plant in which it may or may not exist.

Euxanthone forms pale yellow needle like crystals which melt at 240°. It forms disodium and dipotassium[5] compounds which are red in color. Its monomethyl ether[6] is pale yellow in color and its dimethyl ether is colorless. Other derivatives of euxanthone have been studied by Perkin.[7]

II. A. 1. c.) *Penthydroxy derivatives of diphenyl methanone.*

Maclurin,—Penthydroxy—3, 4, 6, 3′, 4′—diphenyl Methanone.

CH O CH
HOC C— C —C COH
HOC CH HOC COH
CH CH

Maclurin, also called penthydroxy benzophenone and moringa tannic acid, occurs in *Morus tinctoria,*[1] along with morin. Maclurin has been known for a long time and has called forth a large number of investigations. It was first isolated by Wagner[2] in 1850. Wagner considered the substance to be a tribasic acid isomeric with morin. Hlasiwetz and Pfaundler[3] in 1863 recognized the fact that maclurin is not an acid. Bene-

[1] Ann., 51, p. 423.
[2] Jr. prakt. Chem., 33, p. 190.
[3] Ann., 54, p. 265.
[4] Ber., 24, p. 3980; 27, p. 1989.
[5] Ann., 290, p. 156.
[6] Ann., 318, p. 365.
[7] Jr. Chem. Soc., 73, p. 671.
[1] Czapek, II., p. 521.
[2] Jr. prakt. Chem., 51, p. 82; 52, p. 449.
[3] Ann., 127, p. 354; 134, p. 122.

dict[4] in 1877 confirmed the work of Hlasiwetz and Pfaundler. Ciamician and Silber[5] in 1894 attacked the problem of its constitution and partially elucidated its structure. Koenig and Kostanecki[6] in the same year completed this task. Other studies of maclurin have been made by Delffs[7] in 1862; Liebig[8] in 1860; Bedford and Perkin[9] in 1895; and by Perkin in 1897.

Maclurin forms fine pale yellow crystals which melt at 200°. It dissolves in caustic alkalies forming a yellow solution which turns brown upon exposure to the air. Lead acetate gives a yellow precipitate.

Kinoin, — Tetrahydroxy — 3, 4, 5, 3′, — methoxy-4′ — diphenyl methanone.

CH O CH
HOC C — C — C COH
HOC CH HC $COCH_3$
COH CH

Kinoin[1] occurs in the dried juice of *Pterocarpus erinaceus, Pterocarpus marsupium,* and *Coccoloba uvifera,* also in several species of *Eucalyptus,* and in *Butea frondosa.*

In 1879, Etti[2] isolated from green kino a substance which he called kinoin and to which he assigned the formula $C_{14}H_{12}O_6$. This substance contains a hydroxy group and upon hydrolysis yields pyrocatechin and gallic acid. Thomas[3] in his book on the natural dyestuffs has suggested for kinoin the structural formula given above.

A considerable number of investigations of the various species of kino have been made. The results of most of these investigations do not agree with those of Etti, phloroglucin, pyrocatechin,

---

[4] Ann., 185, p. 117.
[5] Ber., 27, p. 1627; 28, p. 1393.
[6] Ber., 27, p. 1996.
[7] Chem. Centrlbl., 1862, p. 284.
[8] Jahresber. d. Chem., 1860, p. 278.
[9] Jr. Chem. Soc., 67, p. 933.
[10] Jr. Chem. Soc., 71, p. 186.
[1] Pharm. Jr., 16, p. 676; Pharm. Ztg., 58, p. 593.
[2] Ber., 11, p. 1876; 17, II, p. 2241.
[3] Les Matieres Colorantes Naturelles, p. 22.

and protocatechuic acid being obtained as the products of hydrolysis.

The principal literature upon kinoin is given in the appended list.

Literature upon kinoin.

Bergholz, Innaug. Dissert. Dorpat.; B., 5, p. 1.
Eissfeldt,—Ann., 134, p. 122.
Etti,—B., 11, p. 1879; 17, p. 2241.
Flueckiger,—B., 17, p. 2241.
Hlasiwetz,—Ann., 134, p. 122.
Kremler,—Pharm. Post., 16, p. 117.
White,—Pharm. Jr., 16, p. 676; 17, p. 702.

Gentisein,—Trihydroxy—2, 4, 3′ —diphenyl methanone oxide, or trihydroxy—, 2, 4, 3′ —xanthone.

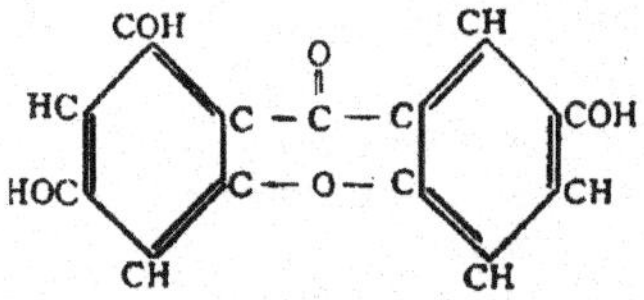

COH O CH
HC C – C – C COH
HOC C – O – C CH
CH CH

Gentisein

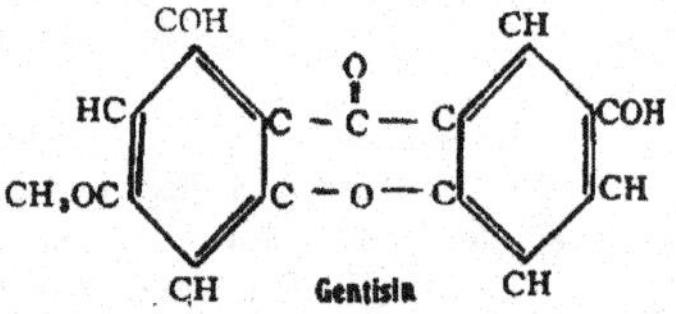

COH O CH
HC C – C – C COH
CH_3OC C – O – C CH
CH CH

Gentisin

Gentisein occurs as its methyl ether gentisin in the rhizome of *Gentiana*[1] *lutea,* also in the rhizome of *Frasera Walteri.* Gentisin was first isolated from the rhizome of *Gentiana lutea* in 1827 by Henry and Caventou. It was studied by Tromsdorff[2] in 1837 and by Le Conte[3] in 1838. Le Conte in his study points out the fact that the gentian plant from which the pigment is obtained, derives its name, according to Pliny, from the Illyrian king Gentis, or Gentius, who appears to have valued the root very highly as a remedy for certain illnesses epidemic in his time. In 1847 Baumert[4] made an extended study of gentisin

[1] Jr. de Pharm., (2) 7, p. 125.
[2] Am. Jr. Pharm., 52, 7.
[3] Jr. de Pharm., (2) 7, p. 178.
[4] Ann., 21, p. 134.

and determined its empirical formula. Hlasiwetz[5] and Habermann, in 1874, took up the study of the constitution of gentisin. In 1876[6] they found that it contains a methoxy group and obtained gentisein by hydrolysis. In 1891 Kostanecki[7] turned his attention to the constitution of gentisin and in 1894[8] succeeded in synthesizing gentisein from phloroglucin and hydroquinone carboxylic acid. From this product he readily obtained gentisin by treatment with methyl iodide. The remaining question of the position of the methoxy group was answered by Perkin[9] in 1898.

Gentisein crystallizes in pale yellow crystals which melt at 315°. It is soluble in alkalies with a bright yellow color.

Gentisin forms fine needle like crystals of a pale yellow color. It forms well defined crystalline salts of sodium and potassium, $C_{14}H_9 NaO_5$ and $C_{14}H_9KO_5$.

II. A. 1. d.) *Hexhydroxy derivatives of diphenyl methanone.*

Datiscetin.

Datiscetin has been known for a long time in southern France where it has been used as a coloring agent for silk. It was first studied by Braconnet[1] in 1816. Later Stenhouse[2] showed that the substance to which the coloring properties are due is a glucoside which may be hydrolized into datiscetin and rhamnose. In 1893 and 1894 Marchlewski[3] and Schunk undertook the determination of the constitution of datiscetin and found that it belongs to the xanthone group of pigments, assigning to it the generally accepted formula $C_{15}H_{12}O_6$ with two hydroxy and two methoxy groups, as shown below. Upon treatment with hydriodic acid datiscetin yields a tetra hydroxy xanthone of a yellow color.

More recently, 1907, Marchlewski[4] claims that datiscetin is of the formula $C_{15}H_{10}O_6$, that it melts at 268°-269° instead of

[5] Ann., 25, p. 200.
[6] Ann., 62, p. 106.
[7] Monats., 12, p. 205; 12, p. 318.
[8] Monats., 15, p. 1; 16, p. 919.
[9] Jr. Chem. Soc., 73, p. 673.
[1] Ann. Chim. et Phys., (2) 3, p. 277.
[2] Ann., 98, p. 167.
[3] Ann., 277, p. 261; 278, p. 346.
[4] Biochem. Zeit., 3, p. 287; Chem. Centralbl., 1906, II, p. 1265.

at 237° as generally given, and that it contains no methoxy groups. Also that it does not reduce Fehling's solution but readily reduces an ammoniacal silver solution, and that it forms tetra acetyl, tetra benzoyl, and tetra benzono sulphonyl derivatives. Furthermore that when the glucoside datiscin is hydrolized, dextrose, not rhamnose is formed. Also that it is an isomer of luteolin and probably a flavone derivative.

COH, HOC, CH_3OC, $COCH_3$, O, C—C—C, C—O—C, CH, CH, CH, CH

Datiscetin

Datiscetin occurs as the glucoside datiscin in *Datisca cannabina.* It crystallizes in clear yellow needle like crystals which melt at 237°.

II. A. 2.) *Pigments referable to phenylethophenyl methane.*

CH, HC, HC, CH, CH, H_2, C—C—C, CH, HC, CH, C CH_2CH_3, CH, CH

Phenyl etho phenyl methane

One pigment of known constitution, catechin, is referable to the above hydrocarbon. Another, cyano maclurin, whose constitution is not yet fully determined is presumably derived from the same hydrocarbon. Cyano maclurin is accordingly placed with catechin in this classification.

Catechin.

```
              CH                    CH
                         OH
                          |
H2C - C           C - CH - C           COH
 |
H2C - C           COH      HC          COH
   \ /
    O         CH                    CH
```

Catechu, also called catechinic acid and catechu tannic acid, was known by Runge[1] to exist in the heart wood of *Acacia catechu* as early as 1821. It has long been known as a dyestuff imparting yellow and brown tints to textile fabrics. The coloring principle, catechin, was probably first described by Nees van Esenbeck[2] in 1832. It has since been the subject of many chemical investigations, the results of which were for a long time so various that the chemistry of catechin remained in a very unsatisfactory condition. The majority of investigators of this pigment have considered but one catechin to exist, some, however, claim that three different catechins with different melting points, but with other properties similar, have been isolated. Perkin,[3] in 1902, described two catechins, with melting points of 175°–176°, and 235°–237° respectively, isolated from *Gambir catechu,* and another with a melting point of 204°–205°, from *Acacia catechu.*

Many different chemical formulae have been assigned to catechin by different chemists. The latest work by Perkin[4] upon this pigment, as well as the even more recent work of Kostanecki[5] and his collaborators, indicates $C_{15}H_{14}O_6$ with five hydroxy groups as the correct formula for the anhydrous compound. Perkin[6] calls attention to the great similarity of the catechins to quercetin, which accompanies them in the plant, probably as a glucoside. He points out the possibility of their being reduction products of quercetin. The later work of Kostanecki and Lampe, however, indicates the presence of a cumaran group, in which the six carbon ring contains only one

[1] Berz. Jahresber., 12, p. 250.
[2] Ann., 1, p. 243.
[3] Jr. Chem. Soc., 81, p. 1160.
[4] Proc. Chem. Soc., 20, p. 177.
[5] Ber., 39, p. 4007, 4014.
[6] Jr. Chem. Soc., 81, p. 1160.

unsubstituted hydrogen instead of the chroman group implied by Perkin's idea. This, they state would make catechin the cumaran derivative of leuco maclurin.

Perkin's suggestion.

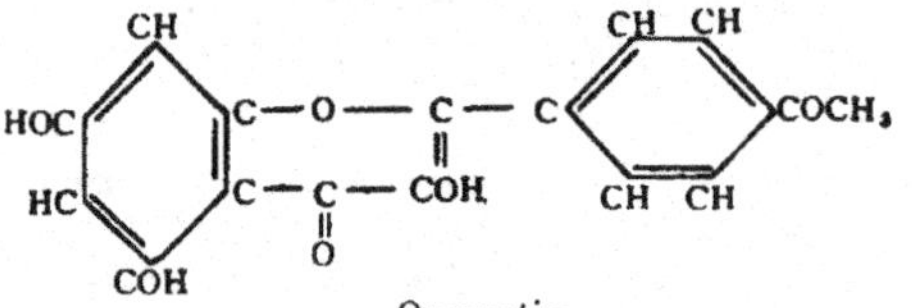

Quercetin

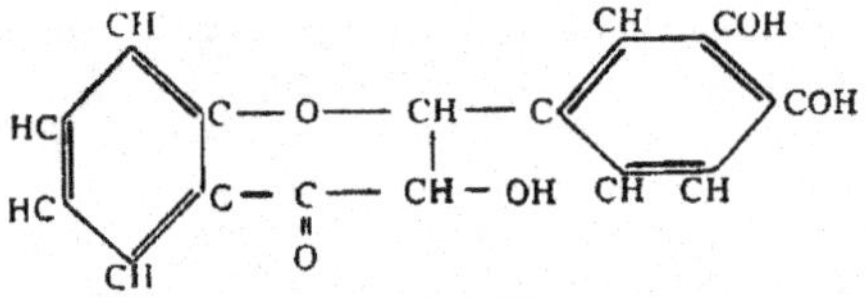

Catechin

Kostanecki's formula.

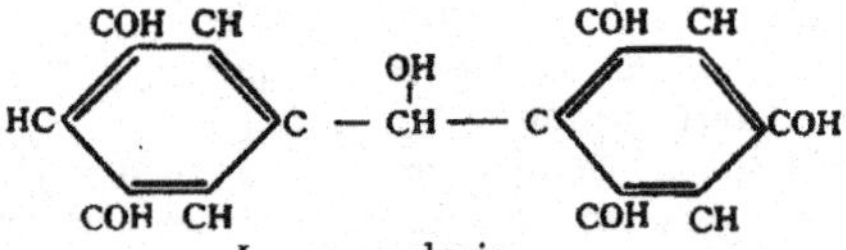

Leuco maclurin

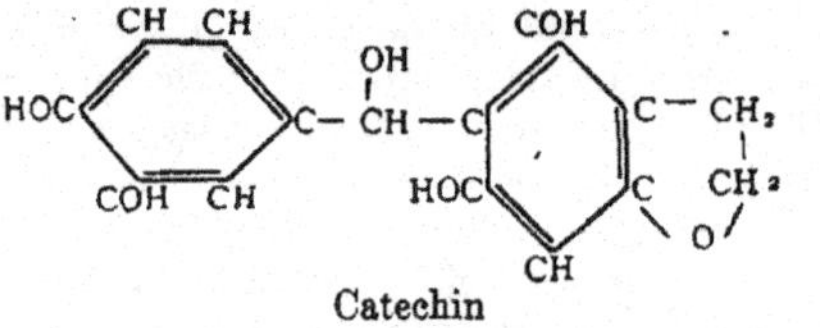

Catechin

Catechin occurs in the heart wood of *Acacia catechu,* in the "Gambir" from *Ouruparia gambir,*[7] and in *Uncaria gambir,*[8]

---

[7] Czapek, II. p. 573.
[8] Jr. Chem. Soc., 81, p. 1160.

also in mahogany wood, and according to Gautier,[9] in various species of cachou, where he thinks there are several varieties of catechin of different melting points and characterized by a varying carbon content.

In a pure state catechin is composed of fine needle like colorless crystals, which by oxidation form dyes imparting yellow shades to textile fabrics. It is sparingly soluble in cold alcohol, readily soluble in hot alcohol. Air dried it dissolves in ethyl acetate, also to some extent in pure ether. Dried at 100° it is insoluble in both these solvents. In aqueous solutions lead acetate gives with catechin a colorless precipitate, ferric salts give a green color. In the presence of sodium acetate ferric chloride gives with catechin a deep violet coloration.

The more important of the contributions to the chemistry of catechin are included in the following list:

Clauser, — B., 36, p. 101.
Dellfs, — Pharm. Centrl., (1846), 604; Berz. Jahresb., 27, p. 284.
Doebereiner, — N. Jahresb. d. Chem. u. Pharm., (1831), p. 378; Berz. Jahresb., 12, p. 250; Schweigg. Jr., 61, p. 378.
Etti, — Monatsh., 2, p. 547; Wien. Akad., 84, p. 553; A., 186, p. 327; Ber., 14, p. 2266.
Gautier, — C. r., 85, p. 342; 86, p. 668.
Hagen, — Ann., 37, p. 320.
Hlasiwetz, — Ann., 134, p. 118.
Kostanecki and Lampe, — B., 39, p. 4007, 4014, 4022; 40, p. 720.
Kraut and Delden, — Ann., 128, p. 285.
Liebermann and Tauchert, — B., 13, p. 964.
Loewe, — Zeit. anal. Chem., 13, p. 113.
Ness van Esenbeck, — Ann., 1, p. 243.
Neubauer, — Ann., 96, p. 337.
Perkin, — Jr. Chem. Soc., 81, p. 1160; Proc. Chem. Soc., 20, p. 177.
Schuetzenberger and Bach, — Bull. Soc. Chem., 4, p. 51.
Swanberg, — Ann., 24, p. 215.
Wackenroder, — Ann., 37, p. 306.
Zwenger, — Ann., 37, p. 320.

[9] C. r., 85, p. 342; 86, p. 668.

Cyanomaclurin

Cyanomaclurin was isolated by Perkin and Cope,[1] in 1895, from *Artocarpus integrifolia,* where it exists along with the yellow pigment morin. Cyanomaclurin crystallizes in colorless crystals which dissolve in sulphuric acid with a beautiful crimson color. Ferric chloride colors an aqueous solution of cyanomaclurin a deep violet color. Dilute alkaline solutions, dissolve it with a deep indigo blue color which on standing changes to green, then brown. It does not combine with mordants to form a dye.

Cyanomaclurin[2] is isomeric with catechin. It is probably a catechin in which the catechol nucleus is replaced by resorcinol.

II. B. *Pigments referable to diphenyl ethane.*

Of the pigments of known constitution only one, Genistein, is believed to be referable to diphenyl ethane.

Genistein.

While the constitution of genistein has not yet been fully determined it is believed by Perkin and Newbury[1] to be represented by the formula

$$(C\,H)_2\,C_6\,H_2 \langle {}^{O}_{C} \rangle CH\,C_6\,H_4\,O\,H \quad (C{=}O)$$

Genistein has been isolated, along with luteolin, from the leaves of *Genista tinctoria.*[2] It crystallizes in colorless needles. To fabrics mordanted with aluminum salts genistein imparts a yellow color.

II. C.) *Pigments referable to diphenyl propane.*

Three pigments, or pigment forming substances, of known constitution are referable to diphenyl propane. These are phloretin, butin, and saponarin or vitexin.

---

[1] Jr. Chem. Soc., 67, p. 939.
[2] Proc. Chem. Soc., 15, p. 179.
[1] Proc. Chem. Soc., 18, p. 138; 20, p. 170.
[2] Jr. Chem. Soc., 75, p. 832; 77, p. 1310.

Phloretin.

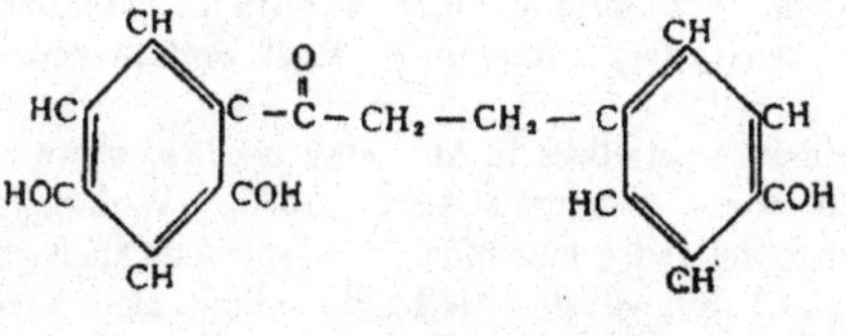

CH CH
O
HC C — C — CH_2 — CH_2 — C CH
HOC COH HC COH
CH CH

Phloretin occurs as the glucoside phloridzin in several species of *Rosaceae,* especially in the leaf buds and the bark of *Pirus malus,*[1] the apple tree. Phloridzin was discovered in 1835 by De Koninck[2] and Stas in the bark of the apple tree. Later Stas,[3] 1839, made an extended study of phloridzin and recognized its glucosidal character, isolating glucose and phloretin. Further studies of phloretin and of phloridzin were made by Rennie,[4] Schiff,[5] Hesse,[6] and Fischer,[7] also by Schunck and Marchlewski.[8] In 1894 Michael[9] found that phloretin upon hydrolysis yields phloroglucin and phloritinic acid. The latter was at the time believed to be p-hydroxy-hydrotropic acid.

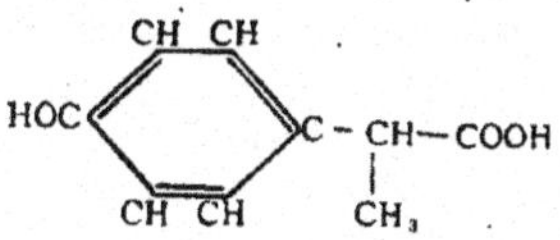

CH CH
HOC C - CH— COOH
CH CH CH_3

Later Bougault[10] found phloretinic acid to be identical with p-hydrocumaric acid.

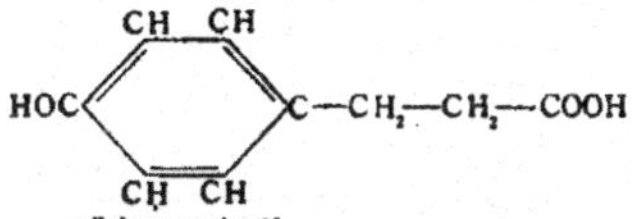

CH CH
HOC C—CH_2—CH_2—COOH
CH CH

p-Hydroxycumaric acid

[1] Jr. Prakt. Chem., 98, p. 205; C. r, 139, p. 294.
[2] Ann., 15, p. 75, 258.
[3] Ann., 30, p. 200.
[4] Jr. Chem. Soc., 49, p. 860; 51, p. 636.
[5] Ann., 172, p. 357; 229; p. 374; B., 2, p. 743; 14, p. 303.
[6] Ann., 176, p. 288.
[7] Ber., 21, p. 288.
[8] Ber., 26, p. 942.
[9] Ber., 27, p. 2686.
[10] C. r., 131, p. 43.

Phloretin crystallizes in small colorless plates. It melts at 253° — 255°. Phloretin forms a tetra-methyl[11] and a tetra-acetyl[12] derivative,[12] therefore must contain four hydroxy groups.

Phloridzin crystallizes in fine silky needles, white or faintly yellow in color. It melts at 108° — 109°. With metals phloridzin forms colored compounds. Conspicuous among these are the dark red iron salt and the bright yellow calcium compound.

Butin,—Trihydroxy—3, 3', 4'—dihydro—α, β—flavone.

CH — CH COH
HOC — C — O — CH — C — COH
HC — C — C — CH_2 — CH CH
CH — O

Butin, a penthydroxy derivative of diphenyl propanone, was first isolated from the flowers of *Butea frondosa* by Hummel and Cavallo[1] in 1894, and later, by Hill[2], in 1903. In 1904 a somewhat extended study of the pigment was made by Perkin[3] who showed that the substance isolated by Hummel and Cavallo and called by them butin was not a single compound but a mixture of two substances, one of which was colorless while the other was orange red in color. The colored substance Perkin named butein, while to the colorless substance he assigned the original name of butin. Perkin showed further that while butin is a trihydroxy dihydro flavanone, butein is a tetrahydroxy derivative of diphenyl propene, benzyliden acetophenone (chalkon). This he proved by the synthesis of butein from monomethyl resacetophenone and dimethyl protocatechinic aldehyde according to the processes of Kostanecki[4] and his colleagues in their synthesis of the chalkon derivatives. After the synthesis of butein, butin was prepared from it by treatment with dilute sulphuric

[11] Ber., 28, p. 1396.
[12] Ber. 27, p. 2686.
[1] Proc. Chem. Soc., 10, p. 11.
[2] Proc. Chem. Soc., 19, p. 133.
[3] Jr. Chem. Soc., 85, p. 1459.
[4] Ber. 37, p. 778, 779, 784.

acid when the compound was, presumably, first hydrated and then dehydrated resulting in a rearrangement of the molecule.

Butin occurs with butein as a glucoside in the blossoms of *Butea frondosa,* a leguminous plant of India and Burma. It crystallizes in small colorless needles melting at 224°–226°. It is soluble in alcohol, sparingly soluble in acetic acid and ether, almost insoluble in benzene. With alcoholic lead acetate solution butin forms a pale yellow precipitate, with alcoholic ferric chloride a deep green coloration. With cold sulphuric acid it first turns red, then goes into solution with a pale yellow color. On fusion with caustic potash and a little water at 200°–220°, butin yileds protocatechuic acid and resorcinol.

Though butin is not itself a pigment it dyes mordanted fabrics exactly as buetin does. From this behavior it is believed that it is changed by the mordants into butein. When boiled with a solution of potassium hydroxide and then acidified a bright orange crystalline precipitate of butein immediately separates out.

Saponarin.

Certain plants contain in the cell sap of the epidermal cells of the leaves a substance which turns blue[1] with iodine. As in the case of starch this color disappears upon heating and returns again upon cooling. For this reason this substance is often mistaken for starch, as it was by its discoverer Sanio[2] in 1857. Schenk,[3] in the same year, doubted the identity of this substance with starch, and Naegeli[4] in 1860 showed that the two are not identical. Dufour,[5] in 1885, found this substance in about twenty species of plants.

In 1906 Barger[6] separated the above described substance from *Saponaria officinalis* and called it saponarin. He showed that the substance is a glucoside which upon hydrolysis yields glucose and another substance $C_{15}H_{14}O_7$, identical with vitexin from *Vitex littoralis.*

The substance which turns iodine blue, formerly known as soluble starch, has been found in *Gagea lutea,*[2] in *Ornithogalum*

[1] Rupe,—Die natuerlichen Farbstoffe, 2, p. 42.
[2] Bot. Zeit., 15, p. 420.
[3] Bot. Zeit., 15, p. 497, 555.
[4] Zeit. fuer. Wissensch. Bot., 2, p. 187.
[5] Bull. Soc. Sci. Nat., 21, p. 227.
[6] Jr. Chem. Soc., 89, p. 1210.

leaves,[7] in *Saponara officinalis,*[8] and in about twenty other species of phanerogams.[5] The identity of the peculiar substance from all these plants with saponarin has not been fully established.

Saponarin forms crystals which, dried in the air, are white, dried in a vacuum they are pale yellow. It is insoluble in cold water, soluble in solutions of caustic alkalies or alkaline carbonates with an intense yellow color. In mineral acids it gives a yellow solution. The solution in sulphuric acid has a blue fluorescence. Upon dilution the saponarin is not precipitated at once. This acid solution, upon the addition of iodine in potassium iodide solution, is colored blue or violet. The glucoside combines with nine acetyl radicals to form a nonacetyl derivative of saponarin.

Vitexin.

Vitexin, $C_{15}H_{14}O_7$, occurs as a glucoside in the New Zealand dye wood *Puriri, Vitex litoralis,*[1] and as the glucoside saponarin in *Saponaria officinalis.*[2]

Vitexin crystallizes in microscopic, glistening plates of a pale yellow color. It melts at 260° with characteristic frothing. It is insoluble in water, slightly soluble in alcohol, soluble in pyridine and in solutions of alkalies with a golden yellow color. Vitexin forms a pentacetyl derivative. Upon treatment with nitric acid it forms a tetranitro apiginin. By decomposition with caustic alkalies it forms phloroglucin and p-hydroxy acetophenone. It is therefore closely related to apiginin from which it differs by the elements of two molecules of water. Since it forms phloroglucin and p-hydroxy benzoic acid the additional hydroxy groups are probably in the pyron cycle, or in a chain which would give rise to this cycle.

```
       CH                                     CH   CH
                              OH
HOC          C  —  O  —  C  —  C                      COH
                              |
HC           C  — CH  — CH  OH                CH   CH
                   |
       COH         OH
```

[7] Bull. Soc. Bot. de France., 5, p. 711.
[1] Jr. Chem. Soc., 73, p. 1019; 77, p. 422.
[2] Jr. Chem. Soc., 89, p. 1210..

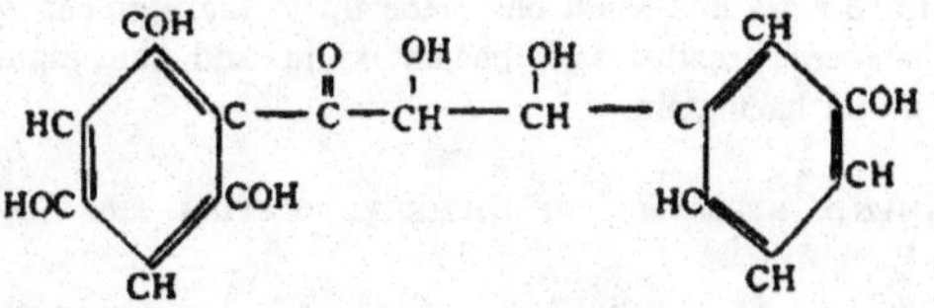

Both the above formulas have, however, six hydroxy groups, whereas vitexin forms only a pentacetyl and saponarin only a nonacetyl derivative. Dehydration might, however, take place in the molecule during the process of acetylation.

To account for the formation of only the pentacetyl vitexin Perkin has suggested the presence of a reduced phloroglucinol nucleus. This would give a formula of the type shown below.

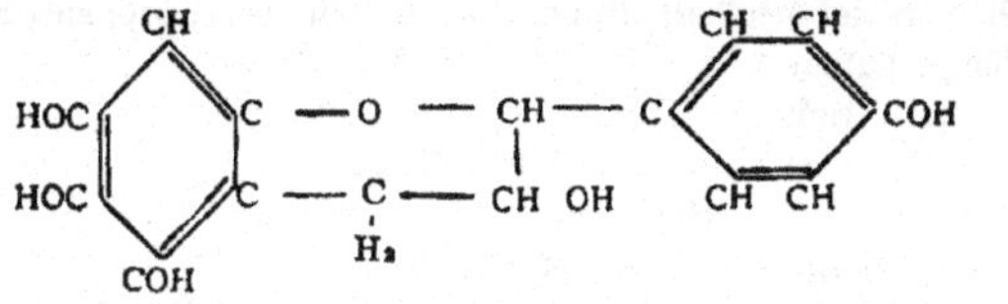

PIGMENTS REFERABLE TO HYDROCARBONS OF THE FORMULA OF SATURATION CH_{2n-16}.

Of all the pigments of known constitution occurring in plants by far the greater number are referable to hydrocarbons of the formula of saturation C_nH_{2n-16}. These pigments when referred to their underlying hydrocarbons fall into three classes.

1.) The diphenyl olefin derivatives.
2.) The dihydroanthracene derivatives.
3.) The methyl-phenyl hydrindine derivatives and their oxidation products.

In the first class are found the flavone derivatives, referable to diphenyl propene, and a large number of compounds referable to similar hydrocarbons. This group also includes the so-called anthocyanine pigments, so far as their structure has been determined.

The second class is made up of the anthraquinone and methyl anthraquinone derivatives, a group which includes, outside of the flavone derivatives, of the above class, the greater number of coloring matters, so far studied, falling under this degree of saturation.

The third class is a small one made up of the pigment forming substances brazilin and haematoxylin and the pigments brazilein and haematein.

I. PIGMENTS REFERABLE TO DIPHENYL OLEFINS AND "HOMOLOGUES."

It was pointed out in connection with the pigments referable to hydrocarbons of the formula of saturation C_nH_{2n-14} that a conspicuously large number of these colored compounds were derivatives of the diphenyl and diphenyl methane series of hydrocarbons. The same relationship is found to exist among the pigments referable to hydrocarbons of the degree of saturation C_nH_{2n-16}, for here we find a considerable number of compounds referable to the diphenyl olefin series of hydrocarbons, having as their initial members diphenyl ethene, diphenyl propene, and diphenyl butene.

A. Diphenyl ethene.
  1.) Tolyl-ethophenyl-ethene.
    Berberin.
B. Diphenyl 1, 3, propene.
  1.) Flavone derivatives.
    Chrysin
      Tectochrysin
    Apiginin
      Acacetin
    Galangin
      Galangin meyhyl ether
    Luteolin
      Luteolin methyl ether
    Lotoflavin
    Fisetin
    Kaempherol
      Kaempherid
    Quercetin
      Rhamnetin
      Isorhamnetin
      Rhamnazin
    Morin
    Myricetin
    Gossypetin

2.) Butein
3.) Anthocyanins.
Pelargonidin
Cyanidin
Paeonidin
Delphinidin
Myrtillidin
Malvidin
Oenidin

C. Diphenyl 1, 4, butene 2.
Indigotin.

I. A. *Pigments referable to the diphenyl ethene series of hydrocarbons.*

1.) The only members of this series to which a plant pigment is referable is a methyl ethyl homologue, the tolyl-etho phenyl-ethene.

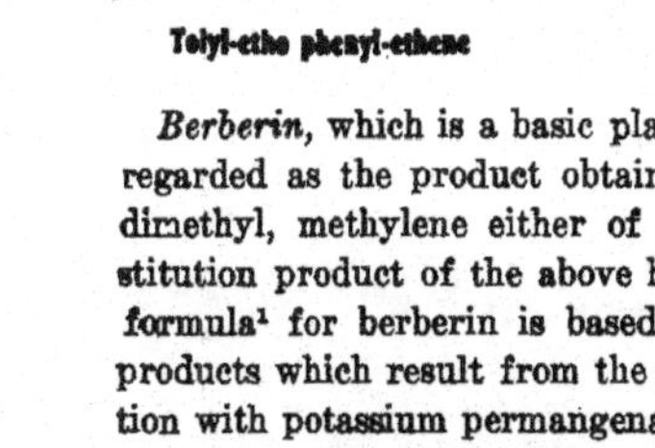

Tolyl-etho phenyl-ethene

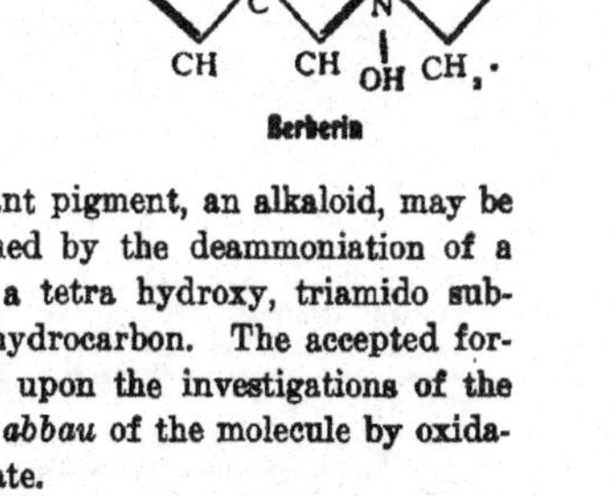

Berberin

Berberin, which is a basic plant pigment, an alkaloid, may be regarded as the product obtained by the deammoniation of a dimethyl, methylene either of a tetra hydroxy, triamido substitution product of the above hydrocarbon. The accepted forformula[1] for berberin is based upon the investigations of the products which result from the *abbau* of the molecule by oxidation with potassium permangenate.

Berberin was isolated by Buchner[2] before 1837 from the root of *Berberis vulgaris* and described by him. Since then it has been the subject of a large number of investigations and has

[1] Jr. Chem. Soc., 55, p. 63; 57, p. 992; 97, p. 818.
[2] Ann., 24 p. 228.

been found to be widely distributed in nature. In addition to several species of barberry it is known to exist in *Hydrastis canadensis*,[3] *Coptis trifola*,[4] *Zanthorrhiza apiifolia*,[5] *Delphinium saniculaefolium*,[6] *Thalictrum flavum*,[7] *Adonis vernalis*,[7] *Mahonia aequifolium*,[8] *Jatrohiza palmata*,[9] *Tintospora rumphii*,[10] *Zylopia polycarpa*,[11] *Chelidonium majus*,[12] *Argemone mexicana*,[13] *Corydalis tuberosa*,[14] *Corydalis vernyi*,[15] *Andria inermis*,[16] *Xanthoxylum caribaeum*,[17] *Xanthoxylum perrottetii*,[18] *Xanthoxylum piperitum*,[19] *Evodia meliifolia*,[20] *Orixa japonica*.[21] Yellow pigments resembling berberin and believed to be identical with it have also been isolated from several other plants.

Berberin crystallizes from water in yellow crystals with six molecules of water of crystallization, from chloroform with one molecule of chloroform of crystallization. It is easily soluble in hot water, difficultly soluble in cold water or chloroform, and almost insoluble in ether, benzene, ligroin, and acetic acid.

A large number of derivatives of berberin have been prepared. It forms salts with acids similar to ammonium salts, also gold and platinum double salts.

Berberin is used for dyeing leather, especially for gloves, also silk and wool.

The following list includes the more important of the many chemical investigations of berberin:

Ahrens,—B., 29, p. 2996.

Bernheimer,—Gazz. Chim. Ital., 13, p. 345.

Buchner and Herbeiger,—Ann., 24, p. 288.

Chevalier and Pelletan,—Jr. Chem. Med., 2, p. 314.

---

[3] Pharm. Z. F. Russl., 33, p. 770; Pharm. Jr. Trans., 3, p. 546.
[4] Arch. Pharm., 222, p. 747.
[5] Pharm. Jr. Trans., 3, p. 546 and 567.
[6] New Commerc. Drugs, 1887; Dragendorff, Heilpflanzen, p. 227.
[7] Monit. Scient., 5, p. 483.
[8] Pharm. Centralh., 1882, nr. 28.
[9] Arch. Pharm., 240, p. 146, 450.
[10] Bull. Inst. Botan. Buitenzorg., 1902, 14, p. 11.
[11] Ann., 105, p. 360.
[12] Am. Jr. Ph., 1902; Botan. Centralbl., 45, p. 187.
[13] Jr. Am. Chem. Soc., 24, p. 238.
[14] Beitr. z. Kennt. d. Corydalis cava., Disser. Dorpat., 1890.
[15] Arch. Pharm., 246, p. 461.
[16] B. Neues. Repert. Pharm., 14, p. 211.
[17] Jr. Chem. Soc., 15, p. 339.
[18] C. r., 98, p. 999.
[19] Dragendorff, Heilpflanzen, p. 350.
[20] Chem. News., 71, p. 207; Arch. Pharm., 213, p. 337.
[21] Nederl. Tijdschr. Pharm., 1884, p. 228.

Dobbie and Lauder,—Proc. Chem. Soc., 17, p. 255.
Fleitmann,—Ann., 59, p. 160.
Freund,—Ann., 397, p. 1.
Freund and Beck,—B., 37, p. 4673.
Freund and Meyer,—B., 40, p. 2604.
Gadamer,—Chem. Ztg., 26, p. 291, 385; Arch. Pharm., 239, p. 648; 243, p. 12, 31, 43, 89, 246.
Gaze,—Beilstein, Handb. organ. Chem., 3, p. 800.
Gordin,—Arch. Pharm., 239, p. 638; 240, p. 146.
Hlasiwetz and Gilm,—Ann., 115, p. 45; 122, p. 256; Suppl. II. p. 133.
Henry,—Ann., 115, p. 133.
Link,—Arch. Pharm., 230, p. 734.
Mosse and Tauz,—Chem. Centralbl., 1901, II. p. 786.
Perkin, A. G.,—Jr. Chem. Soc., 67, p. 413; 71, p. 1189.
Perkin, H. W.,—Jr. Chem. Soc., 55, p. 78; 57, p. 1037.
Perkin, W. H. and Robinson,—Jr. Chem. Soc., 97, p. 305.
Perrins,—Ann., Suppl. II. p. 176.
Schlotterbeck,—Jr. Am. Chem. Soc., 24, p. 238.
Schmidt,—Handb. Organ. Chem., 3rd ed., vol. 2, p. 798.
Troege and Linde,—Arch. Pharm., 238, p. 6.
Weidel,—B., 12, p. 410.

I. B. *Pigments referable to diphenyl—1, 3—propene series of hydrocarbons.*

Just as the larger number of natural coloring matters of the degree of saturation $C_n H_{2n-14}$, may be referred to diphenyl methane, so by far the greater number of those of this degree of saturation, the flavone derivatives, may be referred to a similar hydrocarbon, diphenyl propene. Indeed the relationship of the flavone group to the xanthone group is much closer than would be inferred by simply referring the individual compounds to their underlying hydrocarbons. By comparing the structural formula of xanthone with that of flavone it will be seen that both compounds contain the γ-pyrone group: more than this, they contain the benzo γ-pyrone group, designated by Bloch and Kostanecki[1]. the chromone group. In the xanthone derivatives the chromone group is condensed with another benzene nucleus forming dibenzo γ-pyrone, while in the flavone derivatives it is united with a phenyl group forming phenyl-benzo-γ-pyrone. With this similarity in structure it is by

[1] B., 33, 471.

no means remarkable that flavone and xanthone derivatives so closely resemble each other in coloring properties.

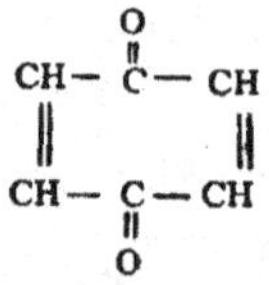

γ-pyrone

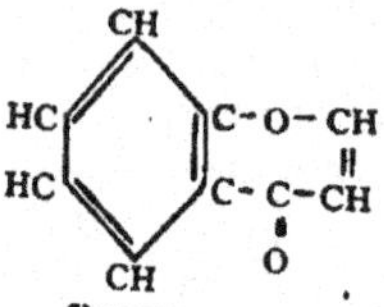

Chromone

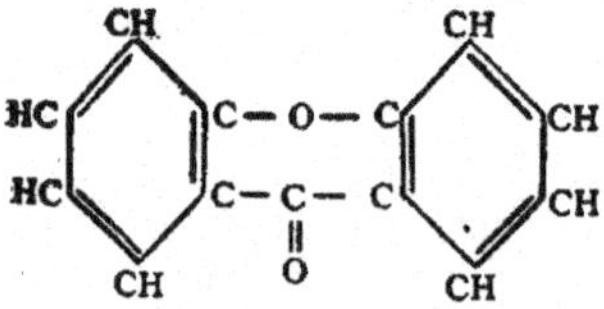

Xanthone

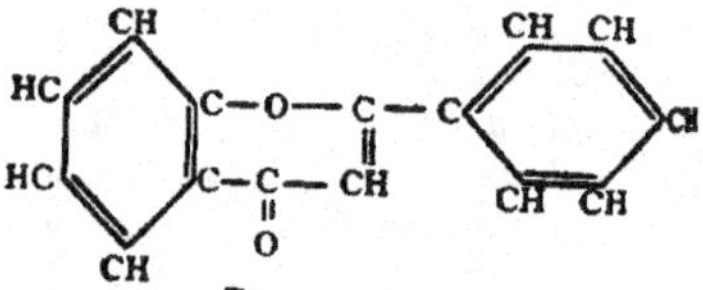

Flavone

There is some confusion as to the numbering of the carbon atoms in the benzo-γ-pyron group, called by Kostanecki the chromon group, and consequently in the numbering of those of the flavon and xanthon groups. According to Richter's *Lexikon der Kohlenstoff-Verbindungen* the oxide oxygen in the chromon group occupies position 1, and the carbon atoms are numbered from this. Kostanecki, however, assigns to the carbon atom adjacent to the carbonyl group the α position and the one adjacent to the oxide oxygen the β position, while the carbon atoms of the carbocyclic nucleus he numbers 1, 2, 3, and 4 respectively. This gives us two systems of numbering as indicated by the following structural formulae:

Chromon group numbered according to

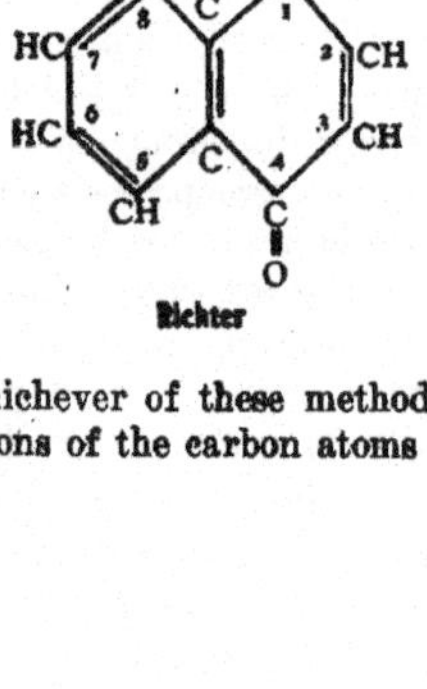

Richter

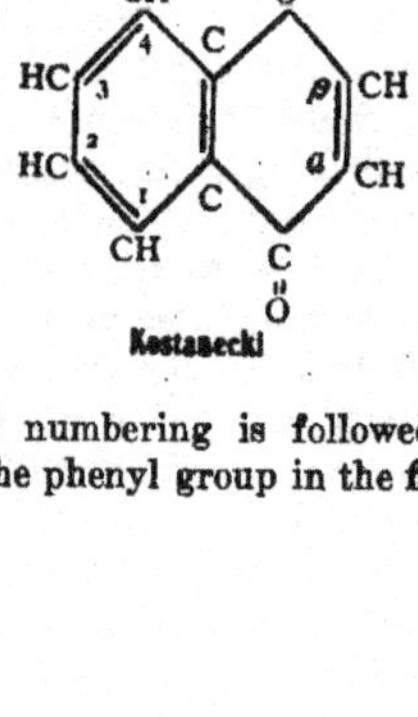

Kostanecki

Whichever of these methods of numbering is followed, the positions of the carbon atoms of the phenyl group in the flavone molecules are 1′, 2′, 3′, 4′, 5′, 6′, beginning with the carbon atom attached to the benzopyron group.

Flavon group numbered according to

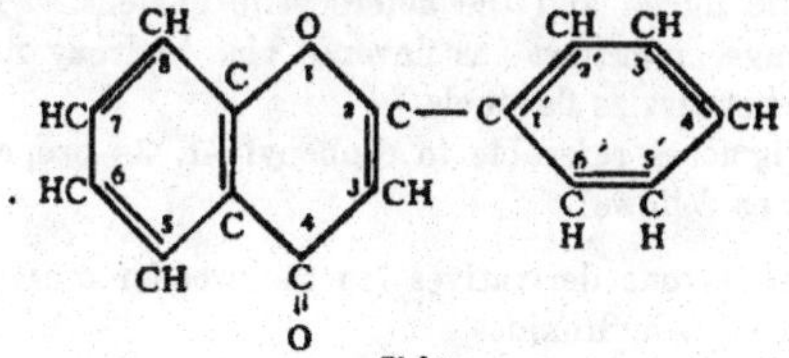

Richter

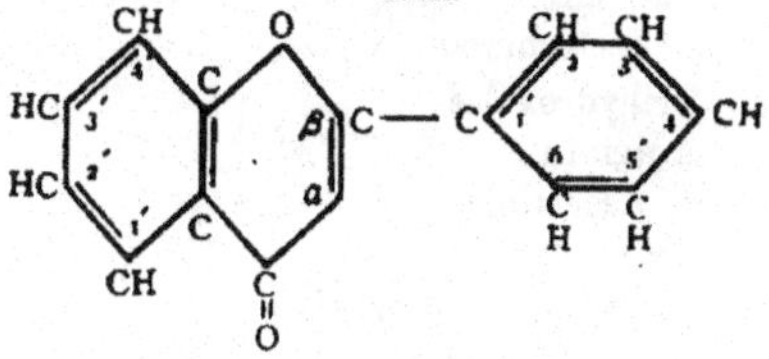

Kostanecki

Though the chromon grouping occurs in the xanthon molecule, as has been shown above, this fact does not seem to be recognized in the outline of cyclic systems as given in Richter's *Kohlenstoff-Verbindugen,* for here an entirely different scheme of numbering is employed for the xanthon grouping.

Xanthon group numbered according to

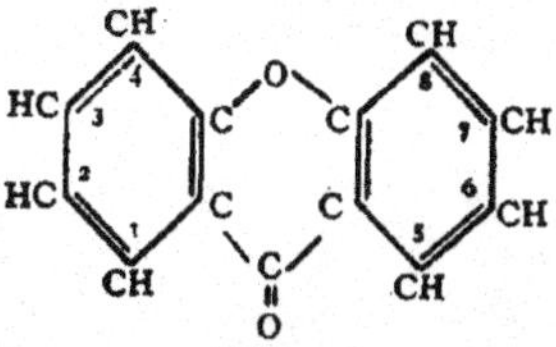

Richter 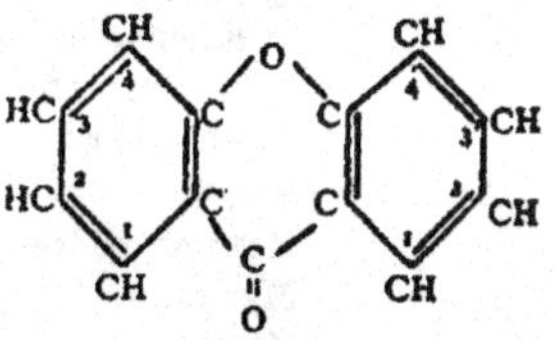 Kostanecki

While it might appear more rational than either of these systems to begin with some differentiated carbon atom and number each succeeding carbon atom in connection with which substitution can take place 1, 2, 3, ...8, 9, 10, etc., without resorting to other symbols yet Kostanecki's method undoubtedly has its advantages since there are three different nuclei in which substitution may take place.

In naming the derivatives of these compound nuclei a distinction is sometimes made between hydroxy derivatives of the carbocyclic nuclei and the heterocyclic nucleus. The former are always regarded as flavones viz. hydroxy flavones, the latter, sometimes as flavonols.

The Pigments referable to diphenyl—1, 3—propene may be classified as follows:

1. The flavone derivatives (in the broader sense.)
   - a.) Dihydroxides.
     - Chrysin.
       - Tectochrysin.
   - b.) Trihydroxides.
     - Apiginin.
       - Acacetin.
     - Galangin.
       - Galangin methyl ether.
   - c.) Tetrahydroxides.
     - Luteolin.
       - Luteolin methyl ether.
     - Lotoflavin.
     - Fisetin.
     - Kaempherol.
       - Kaempherid.
   - d.) Penthydroxides.
     - Quercetin.
       - Rhamnetin.
       - Isorhamnetin.
       - Rhamnazin.
     - Morin.
   - e.) Hexhydroxides.
     - Myricetin.
     - Gossypetin.
2. Butein.
3. Anthocyanin pigments.
   - a.) Tetrahydroxides.
     - Pelargonidin.

b.) Penthydroxides.
Cyanidin.
Paeonidin.
c.) Hexhydroxides.
Delphinidin.
Myrtillidin.
Malvidin.
Oenidin.

Classified with reference to the position of one of the hydroxy groups, i. e. as to whether or not it is in α position thus producing a flavonol group, the flavone pigments, as already pointed out, fall into two classes.

1. The true flavones.
2. The flavonols.

This classification appears desirable inasmuch as Willstaetter looks upon the anthocyanin pigments as related to the flavonols but not to the true flavones.

True Flavones	*Flavonols*
Tetrahydroxides of Chalkon	
Dihydroxy flavones	
Chrysin	
Tectochrysin	
Penthydroxides of Chalkon	
Trihydroxy flavones	Dihydroxy-flavonols
Apiginin	Galangin
Acacetin	Galangin methyl ether
Hexhydroxides of Chalkon	
Tetrahydroxy-flavones	Trihydroxy-flavonols
Luteolin	Fisetin
Luteolin methyl ether	Kaempherol
Lotoflavin	Kaempherid

Hepthydroxides of Chalkon

Tetrahydroxy-flavonols

Quercetin

Rhamnetin

Isorhamnetin

Rhamnazin

Morin

Octhydroxides of Chalkon

Penthydroxy-flavanols

Myricetin

I. B. 1.) *The Flavone Pigments.*

The flavone group constitutes the largest known group of plant coloring matters. All of its members are di-, tri-, tetra-, pent-, and hexhydroxy substitution products of flavone or methyl ethers of these substitution products. Flavone itself is a dehydration product of a hydroxy derivative of diphenyl -1, 3-propene-1-one 3, (chalkone)[1] a compound which is yellow in color and the hydroxy derivatives of which (also yellow in color) have been used for the synthesis of practically of all of the members of this group.

The flavone derivatives are all, as the name indicates, yellow in color. The intensity of the coloration appears to depend somewhat upon both the number and the position of the OH groups and varies from the pale yellow, or almost colorless, apigenin and acacetin to the deep orange yellow myricetin—a hexhydroxy flavone.

The pigments belonging to this group are found in nearly all parts of the plant and both in the free condition and as glucosides. Chrysin, galangin, luteolin and kaempherid are reported as occuring only in the free state; quercetin, fisetin and kaempherol both as such and as glucosides, quercetin being found as the glucosides quercitrin, robinin, rutin, myticolorin, osyritrin. While luteolin is reported only in the free state, its (3) methyl ether occurs as glucoside in the leaves of parsley. All the other members of this group of coloring matters are reported as occurring potentially in the plant as glucosides,

[1] So called by Kostanecki to whose syntheses of the flavone coloring matters we are indebted for much of our knowledge of the structure of these compounds.

While the flavone pigments are found in all parts of the plant they occur most frequently in the roots, wood, bark and leaves. When they appear to be the pigment to which the flower owes its color, the blossoms are either pale yellow or almost white. In some instances, as the occurrence of kaempherol in the blue flowers of *Delphinium consolida* and *Delphinium zali* it is plainly evident that the color is not due to the presence of the flavone derivative but to some other pigment or pigments.

Willstaetter in his work upon anthocyanin has shown that in the *Delphiniums* the color is due to delphinidin, probably a potassium salt of delphinidin. Delphinidin, according to Willstaetter, is isomeric with quercetin and morin, both of which are hydroxy substitution products of kaempherol.

The flavone derivatives are not quinoid in character. All can be, however, theoretically, and some have been, actually, oxidized to quinoidal compounds (See chrysin[2] and quercetin.[3]). These quinones are deep red in color and closely resemble, in their behavior toward reagents, the red and blue pigments of flowers (anthocyanins). These quinones can be reduced to the corresponding hydroquinones which form either colorless or pale yellow crystals.

From a consideration of the above reactions, also as a result of observations upon the distribution of anthocyanin, and from experimental evidence on the concentration of sugars and glucosides in various tissues, on the existence of enzymes, and on sugar feeding, there has recently been formulated a hypotheses (Miss Muriel Wheldale[4]) that: The soluble pigments in flowering plants, termed anthocyanin, are oxidation products of colorless chromogens, existing in the tissues as glucosides. The production of the glucoside from the chomogen and sugar is in the nature of a reversible enzyme reaction: chromogen + sugar = glucoside + water, and the oxidation of the chromogen, which is effected by one or more enzymes, can take place only after its liberation from the glucoside.

According to Miss Wheldale this hypothesis brings the formation of anthocyanine into line with that of pigments formed after the death of the plant (indigotin etc.) It is not opposed to the quinhydrone hypothesis of pigmentation and it is in ac-

---

[2] Ber., 45, 499.
[3] Ber., 44, 3487.
[4] Jr. Genetics, 1, 133, (Jr. Chem. Soc., A. II, 80).

cord with the observations of Kastle[5] and Hayden on the blue coloring matter of chicory blossoms. It is not in harmony, however, with the recent work of Willstaetter upon anthocyanins. According to Willstaetter it ought to be possible to produce anthocyanins by the reduction (not oxidation) of quercetin or other flavonols. Such an anthocyanin would be, not the quercetone or similar quinone of Niernstein and Wheldale, but an oxonium compound of a reduced quercetin or other flavonol.

Dihydroxy flavones

Chrysin,—Dihydroxy-1, 3-Flavone.

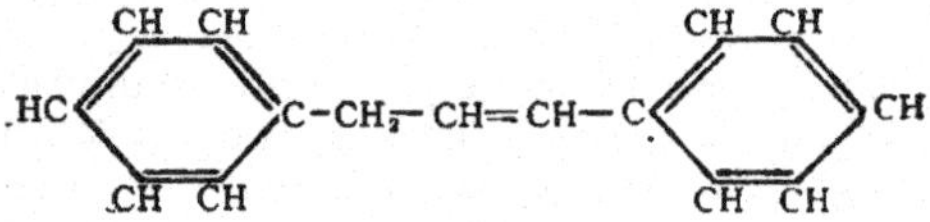

Diphenyl-1, 3-propene

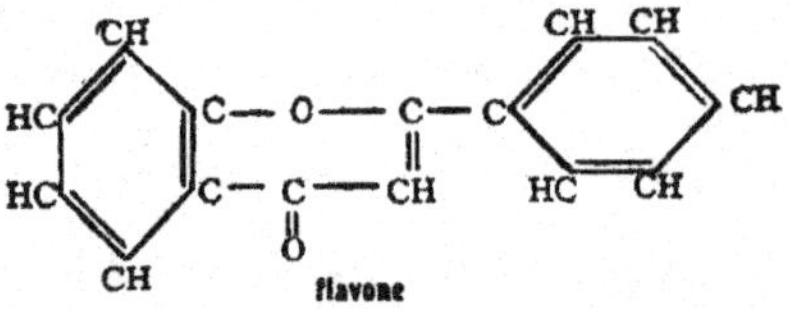

flavone

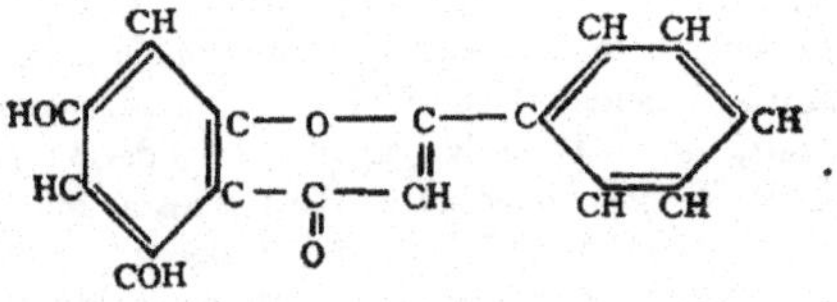

Dihydroxy — 1, 3-flavone

Chrysin was probably first isolated by Hallwachs[1] in 1857 from the buds of *Populus nigra* or *Populus dilatata*. In 1864 Piccard[2] extracted chrysin from several varieties of poplar where he found it in the growing leaf buds. He named it "*chrisinsaeure*" to indicate both its yellow color and its salt forming properties. Several years later Piccard[3] undertook

[5] Am. Chem. Jr., 46, 315.
[1] Ann., 101, p. 372.
[2] Jr. f. Prakt. Chem., 93, p. 369.
[3] Ber., 6, p. 884; 7, p. 888; 10, p. 176.

a study of chrysin. In a series of articles he described its principal properties and attacked the problem of its constitution. This was determined later by Kostanecki[4] and his associates. (1893–1904) The work of Kostanecki was confirmed by that of Darier[5] in 1895.

Our present conception of the constitution of chrysin is based upon its decomposition by caustic alkalies into phloroglucin, acetic acid and benzoic acid, with small quantities of acetophenone. Also upon its synthesis from phloracetophenone trimethyl ether and ethyl benzoate.

Chrysin occurs in the buds of many species of poplar, including *Populus pyramidalis,*[6] *Populus nigra,*[7] *Populus monolifera,*[8] and *Populus balsamifera.*[9]

Chrysin forms clear yellow crystals. It melts at 275 and sublimes in fine needles at a temperature a little above the melting point. It is insoluble in water but soluble in both hot and cold alcohol, in aniline and acetic acid. It is difficultly soluble in ether and almost insoluble in carbon disulphide. In alkaline solutions it dissolves with a yellow color. Chrysin is precipitated from alcoholic solutions by lead acetate but dissolves in an excess of the reagent.

Treated with chromic acid and acetic acid chrysin is oxidized to chrysone,[10] a red amorphous powder which crystallizes in deep red needles melting above 360. Chrysone is insoluble in the ordinary organic solvents. It dissolves in concentrated sulphuric acid with a red color, in alkalies with a blue color. It forms a monoacetyl derivative which crystallizes in red needles. The acetyl derivative when reduced with zinc and acetic acid anhydride forms a white acetylated hydroxychrysin which, when hydrolized, crystallizes in small crystals melting at 304–305.

Tectochrysin, a methyl ether of chrysin.

Tectochrysin[11] was first obtained by Piccard in the purification of chrysin. He called it tectochrysin from a Greek word

[4] Ber., 26, p. 2901; 32, p. 2260, 2449; 37, p. 3167.
[5] Ber., 27, p. 21.
[6] Ber., 6, p. 884.
[7] Ann., 101, p. 372.
[8] Ber., 6, 890; 7, p. 1485.
[9] Ber., 16, p. 176.
[10] Ber., 45, p. 499.
[11] Ber., 6, p. 888.

which means fusible, because its melting point is much lower than that of chrysin. Tectochrysin may be prepared synthetically by treating chrysin in alcoholic solution with methyl iodide. It is more readily soluble than chrysin, being easily soluble in benzine (distinction from chrysin.) Tectochrysin is sulphur yellow in color.

Trihydroxy flavones

Apigenin,—Trihydroxy—1, 3, 4'—flavone.

CH, HOC, HC, COH, C—O—C—C, C—C—CH, O, CH CH, COH, CH CH

Apigenin

The glucoside apiin, of which apiginin is a component, seems to have been first isolated by Rump[1] in the course of his work on the chemical analysis of *Apium petroselinum*, but it was not until 1843 that Braconnot[2] first hydrolised this glucoside. Braconnot also applied the name apiin to the glucoside but made no analysis of the products of hydrolysis. In 1850 Planta and Williams[3] analysed apigenin and described it under the name of pure apiin. In 1867, Lindenhorn[4] showed the glucosidal character of apiin, and that by hydrolysis it gave glucose and a new substance to which he gave the name apigenin. Gerichten,[5] in 1876, took up the study of the constitution of apigenin, basing his conclusions upon its decomposition in the presence of alkalies. He ascribed to apigenin the formula $C_{15}H_{10}O_5$, a formula which has since been verified by the work of Perkin,[6] and more recently by that of Kostanecki and Tambor.[7]

Apigenin occurs as the glucoside apiin in *Petroselinum*

[1] Rep. f. Pharm., 6, p. 6.
[2] Ann. d. Phys. et Chim., 9, p. 250.
[3] Ber., 9, p. 112.
[4] Innaug. Dissert. Wuerzburg, 1867.
[5] Ber., 9, p. 259, 1121, 1477.
[6] Jr. Chem. Soc., 71, p. 807; 77, p. 420.
[7] Ber., 33, p. 1990.

sativum, Apium graveolens, and perhaps in other unbelliferous species.

Apigenin forms crystals of a pale yellow color which melt at 212–215. It is difficultly soluble in water and in ether, more readily in alcohol. Alkalies dissolve it with a yellow color. In alcoholic solution it yields with lead acetate a yellow precipitate, with ferric chloride a red brown coloration.

Acacetin, a monomethyl ether of apigenin was named by Perkin[1] who first obtained it from the leaves of *Robina pseudacacia.*

Acacetin occurs in the leaves of the false acacia, *Robina pseudacacia.* It forms almost colorless needle like crystals which dissolve in alkaline solutions with a pale yellow color. From alcoholic solutions it is precipitated by lead acetate. With ferric chloride it gives a reddish brown color. It forms a diacetyl derivative which crystallizes in colorless needles which melt at 195–198. Fused with alkalies, acacetin yields phloroglucin and parahydroxybenzoic acid.

Galangin,—Trihydroxy—1, 3, —flavone or

Dihydroxy—1, 3—flavonol.

CH CH CH
HOC C — O — C — C CH
HC CH- C — COH CH CH
COH O

Galangin was first obtained by Brandes,[1] in 1839, together with kaempferid, from *Galanga* root, *Alpinia officinarum.* It was not, however, recognized by him as a distinct compound, and it was not until Jahns,[2] in 1881 showed that the kaempferid of Brandes was composed of a mixture of three substances which he called kaempferid, galangin, and alpinin, that galangin was actually isolated. In a later study (1900) of the colored compounds of *Galanga* root, Testoni[3] met with nothing correspond-

[1] Proc. Chem. Soc., 16, p. 45; Jr. Chem. Soc., 77, p. 430.
[1] Arch. der Pharm., (2) 19, p. 52.
[2] Ber., 14, pp. 2305 and 2807; Arch. der Pharm., 220, p. 161.
[3] Gazz. chim. ital., 30, (2) p. 327.

ing to the alpinin of Jahns, but found a methyl ether of galangin.

Jahns in his study of the constitution of galangin found its formula to be $C_{15}H_{10}O_5$, also that it has three hydroxy groups, and that upon fusion with potassium hydroxide it yields benzoic acid, oxalic acid and a phenol like substance. Kostanecki[4] and his associates by the hydrolysis, and subsequent synthesis of galangin, established its formula as given above.

Galangin crystallizes in yellowish white needles which melt at 214–215, and sublime with partial decomposition. It is almost insoluble in water, easily in ether, slightly in chloroform and benzene. It dissolves in alkalies with a yellow color. It yields a triacetyl and a tri methyl derivative, the latter, treated with acetic acid, yields a monoacetyl compound.[5]

Galangin methyl ether.

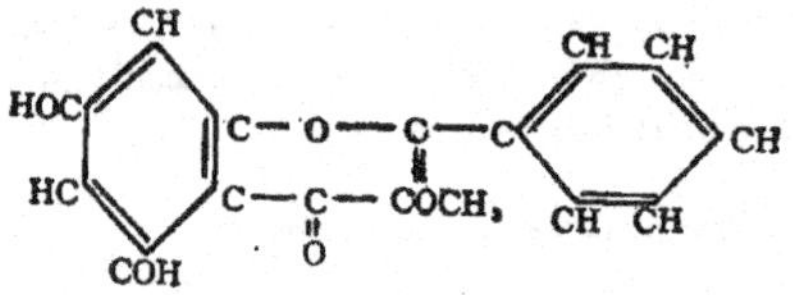

A galangin methyl ether, probably with the methyl group in the position indicated above,[6] occurs along with galangin in the root of *Alpinia officinarum.*[7]

Tetrahydroxy flavones.

Luteoline,—Tetra hydroxy—1, 3, 3′, 4′—flavone.

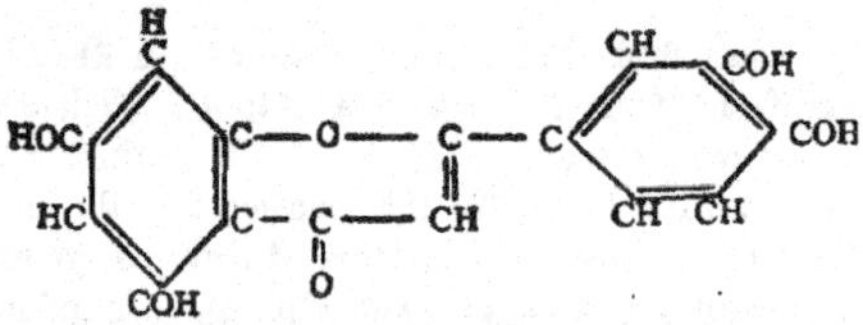

Luteoline was first isolated by Chevreul,[1] in 1830, and named by him from its source, *Reseda luteola*. Since that time it has been

[4] Ber., 37, p. 2803.
[5] Ber., 14, p. 2807.
[6] Czapek, Biochemie der Pflanzen, vol. 2, p. 523.
[7] Gazz. chim. ital., 30 (2) p. 327.
[1] Jr. Chim. Med. 6, p. 157.

studied by a number of chemists, Moldenhauer,[2] Schuetzenberger[3] and Paraf, Halsiwetz[4] and Pfaundler, Roechleder,[5] Adrian[6] and Trillot, Herzig,[7] Perkin,[8] and Kostanecki.[9]

Our present conception of the constitution of luteoline, like that of the other members of the flavone group, is based upon its decomposition by alkaline fusion when it yields phoroglucine and protocatechuic acid. Perkin, therefore ascribed to luteoline the foregoing formula which has since been verified by the synthesis, effected by Kostanecki[10] and his associates, of luteolin from phloracetophenone trimethyl ether and the diethyl ether of dihydroxy—3, 4—benzoic acid.

Luteoline occurs, as such, in *Reseda*[11] *luteola* in the leaves of *Digitalis*[12] *purpurea,* and in *Genista*[13] *tinctoria.* The 3-methyl ether of luteoline occurs as a glucoside in the leaves of parsley, *Petroselium sativum.*

Luteoline forms small quadrangular needles of a yellow color and bitter, astringent taste. They melt at 350° and sublime with partial decomposition. They are slightly soluble in cold water, better in warm water, alcohol, ether, and warm acetic acid.

Dry luteoline treated with phosphoric acid anhydride is changed to a red substance which dissolves in ammonia with a violet coloration. The aqueous solution of luteoline is colored first green, then reddish brown by ferric chloride, olive green by copper acetate. Luteoline dissolves in concentrated sulphuric acid with an orange red color and is precipitated unchanged by dilution. If to a saturated solution of luteolin in boiling acetic acid sulphuric acid is added, small orange red crystals, insoluble in acetic acid and decomposed by water into luteoline and sulphuric acid, are formed. Hydrobromides are formed in a similar manner with hydrobromide acid.

---

[2] Jr. Prakt. Chem., 70, p. 428.
[3] Bull. Soc. Chim., (1) p. 1861–18.
[4] Ann., 112, p. 107.
[5] Zeit. Anal. Chem. (1886) p. 602.
[6] C. r., 129, p. 889.
[7] Ber., 29, 1013; Monats., 17, p. 926.
[8] Jr. Chem. Soc., 69, p. 206, p. 1439.
[9] Ber., 32, p. 1184; 34, 1458; 37, 2625.
[10] Ber., 33, p. 3415.
[11] Ann., 100, p. 150; Jares., (1861) p. 707.
[12] Arch. Pharm., 388, p. 313; B., 32, p. 1184.
[13] Euler (1), p. 105.

Luteolin methyl ether is found as a glucoside in the green herb of parsley.

Lotoflavin,—Tetrahydroxy—1, 3, 2', 4'—flavone.

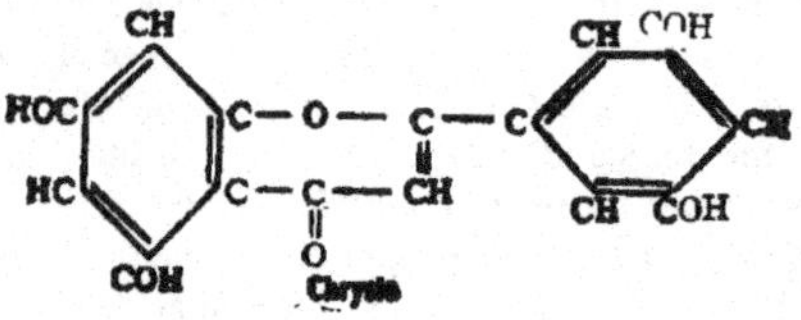

Lotoflavin was first met with in 1900 by Dunstan[1] in *Lotus arabicus,* a small leguminous plant growing abundantly in Egypt. This plant, which very closely resembles the common vetch, is commonly known as kuther. From the fact that fused with alkalies it yields β-resorcylic acid and phloroglucin, Dunstan and Henry[2] conclude that the structure of lotoflavin is as above.

Lotoflavin occurs in the *Lotus arabicus* in the form of a glucoside, lotosin, which by the action of dilute acids, or of a special enzyme, lotase, is hydrolised yielding lotoflavin, sucrose, and hydrocyanic acid.

Lotoflavin is a yellow crystalline substance readily soluble in alcohol or hot glacial acetic acid. It dissolves also in alkalies with a bright yellow color. It does not combine with mineral acids, but it forms a triacetyl derivative and two isomeric trimethyl ethers. By the action of fused alkalies it is converted into phloroglucin and resorcylic acid.

Fisetin,—Tetrahydroxy a—3', 4', a—flavone, or Trihydroxy—3, 3', 4' flavonol.

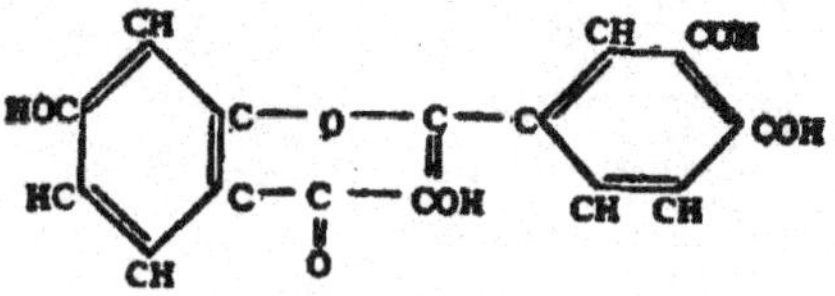

[1] Proc. Roy. Soc., 67, p. 224; 68, p. 374.
[2] Chem. News., 8, p. 301; 84, p. 26.

Chevreul[1] probably first extracted fisetin in the form of a tannin, though perhaps impure, from the fustel wood. Some years later it was again obtained from the same source by Bolley.[2] It was later isolated and studied by Schmidt,[3] Herzig,[4] Perkin,[5] and Kostanecki.[6]

Our ideas of the constitution of fisetin are based upon the work of Hirzig who showed that by boiling with alcoholic potassium hydroxide fisetin did not yield phloroglucin, but fisetol and protocatechuic acid, with traces of resorcin. By the synthesis of fisetol (ethylresorcylic acid), Kostanecki and Tambor confirmed the work of Herzig.

COC_2H_5

HC CH

HC COH

C

COOH

Fisetol.

Fisetin occurs as a glucoside in *Rhus cotinus,*[7] *Rhus rhodanthema,*[8] and *Quebracho colorado.*[9] It also occurs free in *Rhus rhodanthema,*[10] and in the blossoms of *Butea frondosa.*[11]

Crystallized from dilute alcohol fisetin forms small lemon yellow needle like crystals. From acetic acid it crystallizes in yellow prisms with six molecules of water of crystallization.

Fisetin is almost insoluble in water, easily soluble in alcohol, acetone and acetic acid. It is difficultly soluble in ether, benzene, petroleum ether and chloroform. Ferric chloride when added to fisetin solutions produces a dark green coloration and

[1] Zeit. anal. Chem., 12, p. 127.
[2] Bull. Soc. Chim., 2, p. 479.
[3] Ber., 19, p. 1734.
[4] Monatsh., 12, p. 177.
[5] Jr. Chem. Soc., 67, p. 648; 69, p. 1304.
[6] Ber., 28, p. 2302; 37, p. 784; 38, p. 3587.
[7] Ber., 19, p. 1703.
[8] Jr. Chem. Soc., 71, p. 1194.
[9] Chem. News, 74, p. 120.
[10] Jr. Chem. Soc., 71, p. 1194.
[11] Proc. Chem. Soc., 19, p. 183; Jr. Chem. Soc., 85, p. 1459.

upon the addition of ammonia, a black precipitate. Lead acetate added to fisetin solutions forms an orange yellow precipitate which is easily soluble in acetic acid.

Fisetin forms tetramethyl, tetraethyl, tetrabenzoyl, and tetraacetyl derivatives. By fusion with alkalies it yields phloroglucin, resorcinol, and protocatechuic acid. Treated with chromic acid[12] it does not yield an oxidation product corresponding to those produced from chrysin and quercetin under the same condition. To fabrics mordanted with aluminum fisetin imparts an orange color, with tin a bright red or yellow red color, with chromium a brown color.

Kaempherol,—Tetrahydroxy a—1, 3, 4',—flavone, or—Trihydroxy—1, 3, 4'—flavonol.

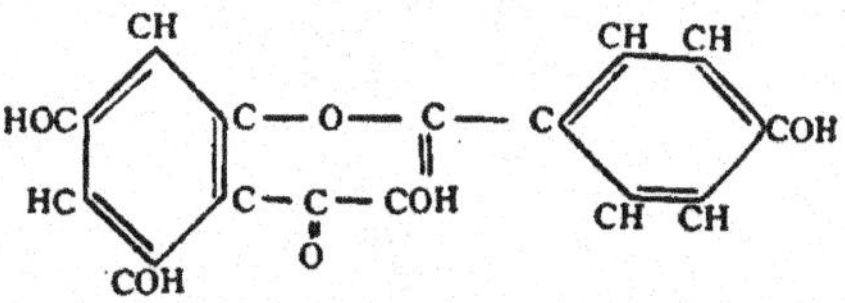

Kaempherol was probably first extracted by Zwenger[1] and Dronk, in 1861, as the glucoside robinin from *Robinia pseudacacia.* It was considered by them, however, to be a glucoside of quercetin. It was first prepared from kaempherid, its 3-methyl ether, in 1897 by Gordin[2] who treated the crystalline kaempherid with strong hydriodic acid solution thus securing the free kaempherol. It was later isolated by Perkin (1900) from the flowers of *Delphinium consolida*[3] and by him identified. Perkin also isolated the glucoside robinin from the flowers of *Robinia pseudacacia.*[4] The constitutional formula of kaempherol follows from its preparation from kaempherid, and from its synthesis, along with that of kaempherid, by Kostanecki and others.

Kaempherol occurs both as such and combined as the gluco-

---

12 Ber., 45, p. 499.
1 Ann., Sup. 1, (1861) p. 257.
2 Ber., 34, p. 3723.
3 Jr. Chem. Soc., 81, p. 585.
4 Proc. Chem. Soc., 17, p. 87.

side in the blue flowers of *Delphinium consolida*[5] and *Delphinium zali*,[6] as the glucoside in the white flowers of *Robinia pseudacacia*,[7] and, along with quercetin in the blossoms of *Prunus spinosa*,[8] *Alpina officinarum*,[9] and *Rumex eckonianus*.[10] It has also been isolated from the indigo producing plants,[11] *Polygonum tinctorium* and *Indigofera amicta*, as the glucoside kaempheritrin. Scutellarein,[12] probably identical with kaempherol, is formed by the hydrolysis of the glucoside scutellarin which occurs in the epidermis of *Scutellaria caleopsis*, and *Teucrium* species.

Kaempherol crystallizes in pale yellow crystals which melt at 276–277. It is readily soluble in boiling alcohol, and soluble in alkalies with a pale yellow color. Alcoholic lead acetate solutions yield an orange red precipitate with kaempherol; alcoholic ferric chloride a greenish black coloration. Kaempherol dissolves in concentrated sulphuric acid forming a yellow solution which in a short time gives a blue fluorescence. To wools mordanted with aluminum kaempherol imparts a yellow color; with tin, a yellow color; with chromium, a brownish red color; and with iron, a deep olive brown.

Kaempherid,—Trihydroxy—1, 3, a-methoxy-4'-flavone, or Dihydroxy-1, 3-methoxy-4'-flavonol.

```
        CH              CH  CH
HC          C—O—C—C              COCH3
                |
HC          C—C—COH     CH  CH
              ||
              O
        COH
```

Kaempherid, the 4'-methyl ether of kaempferol, was first extracted by Brandes[1] in 1839 from the rhizom of *Alpina officinarum*. Later, as has been shown in the chapter on galangin,

[5] Jr. Chem. Soc., 81, p. 585.
[6] Jr. Chem. Soc., 73, p. 267.
[7] Proc. Chem. Soc., 20, p. 172.
[8] Ann. (Sup.) 1, p. 257.
[9] Arch. d. Pharm., 247, p. 447.
[10] Jr. Chem. Soc., 97, p. 1.
[11] Jahresb. d. Chem., (1886) p. 573; Proc. Chem. Soc. 20, p. 172; 22, p. 198.
[12] Euler, p. 105.
[1] Arch. der Pharm., 67, p. 52.

this kaempferid of Brandes was found by Jahns[2] to be a mixture of three substances which he called kaempferid, galangin, and alpinin. Our ideas of the constitution of kaempferid, and also of kaempferol, are based upon its behavior with oxidizing substances and alkalies. By the action of oxidizing agents it yields para hydroxy benzoic acid and oxalic acid, fused with alkalies, oxalic acid, formic acid, and phloroglucine.

This conception of the formulas of kaempferid and kaempferol is supported by the work of Kostanecki[3] and his associates, also by that of Gordin,[4] and of Cimician and Silber,[5] and it is confirmed by its synthesis by Kostanecki, Lampe and Tambor.[6] In this synthesis hydroxy-2′-trimethoxy-4′, 6′, 4-chalkon,[7] synthesized from phloracetophenone-dimethyl ether and anise aldehyde, treated in alcoholic solution with dilute sulphuric acid, yielded trimethoxy-1, 3, 4′-flavonon, which in turn gave the trimethoxy-1, 3, 4′-flavonol, and that gave the trihydroxy—1, 3, 4′—flavonol.

Kaempherid occurs, as has been already pointed out, in the rhizom of *Alpina officinarum*.

Kaempferid crystallizes in yellow plates which melt at 224–225. It is insoluble in water, slightly soluble in cold alcohol, chloroform and benzene, readily soluble in hot alcohol, ether, and sulphuric acid. It dissolves with an intense yellow color in solutions of the alkalies and the alkaline carbonates. In concentrated sulphuric acid it dissolves with a yellow color and a blue fluorescence. The alcoholic solution gives an olive green precipitate with ferric chloride, and a yellow precipitate with lead acetate. It reduces Fehling's solution when warmed.

---

[2] Ber., 14, p. 2305, 2807; Gazz. chim ital., 30 (11) p. 327.
[3] Ber., 32, p. 318; 34, 3723; 28, p. 2302.
[4] Ber., 34, p. 3723; Dissertation, Berne, 1897.
[5] Ber., 32, p. 861.
[6] Ber., 37, p. 2096.
[7] Ber., 37, p. 192.

Penthydroxides of flavone.

Quercetin,—Penthydroxy—1, 2, 3', 4', α-flavone, or Tetrahydroxy—1, 2, 3', 4' -flavonol.

[structural formula: HOC, HC, CH, C—O—C—C, COH, C=O, OH; CH, COH, COH, CH CH]

Quercetin which occurs very widely distributed throughout the plant kingdom, both in the free state and as a glucoside, has probably been more widely studied than any other vegetable coloring matter except chlorophyll and, perhaps indigo and alizarin. Quercetin was first extracted as a glucoside quercitrin by Chevreul[1] from the inner bark of *Quercus tinctoria* and later from the same source, also from the horse chestnut, by Rochleder.[2] The free quercetin was first obtained from the glucoside by Rigaud,[3] in 1854. The names of the various chemists who have since contributed to the literature of quercetin, with references to their published works are given in the appended list, which, although it contains the more important articles upon quercetin, is probably not at all complete.

Our conception of the structure of quercetin comes from the work of Hirzig,[4] also that of Kostanecki[5] and his associates. Fused with alkalies it yields phloroglucin, Protocatehuic acid, and glycolic acid.

$$C_{15}H_{10}O_7 + 3H_2O = C_6H_3(OH)_3 + C_6H_3(OH)_2COOH + CH_2OH\,COOH.$$

Quercetin has been synthesized by Kostanecki and his collaborators in a manner quite similar to their synthesis of fisetin.[6]

Quercetin occurs very widely distributed in the free state, as alkyl ethers, and as glucosides. As a glucoside it is most

---

[1] Leçons de Chemie appliquée à la Teinture.
[2] Wien. Acad. Ber., 33, p. 565.
[3] Ann., 90, p. 283.
[4] Monatsh., 12, p. 177; 14, p. 38.
[5] Ber., 37, p. 784, 793.
[6] Ber., 37, p. 784, 793.

frequently met with combined with rhamnose though it often combines with other sugars, sometimes forming mixed glucosides with one or more molecules of rhamnose and one or more of another sugar, glucose or galactose.

As a glucoside quercetin is found in the bark of *Quercus tinctoria, Q. digitata,* or *Q. trifida,*[7] in the bark of *Carya tomentoria,*[8] in grape leaves,[9] *Viola tricolor,*[10] leaves of *Eucalyptus macrorrhyncha,*[11] leaves of *Ruta graveolens,*[12] buds of *Sophora japonica,*[13] leaves of *Colpoon compressum,*[14] *Arctostaphylos uva ursa,*[15] in North American *Chimaphila* species,[16] in *Calluna vulgaris,*[17] in the blossoms of *Tagetes patula,*[18] in horse chestnut,[19] in the leaves and blossoms of *Cherianthus cheri*[20] and of *Crataegus oxycanthus,*[21] in the blossoms of *Viola tricolor var. evensis,*[22] and in the blossoms of the cotton plant.[23]

In its free state quercetin has been found by Perkin[23] in *Rhamnus* (fruit), *Hippophae* (berries), *Rhus cotinus* (bark), Apple (bark), *Prunus spinosa* (blossoms), *Aesculus* (leaves and flowers), *Cornus* (flowers), Grape (leaves), *Allium cepa, Podophyllum,* and the fruit of *Rumex obtusifolia.*[24] It has been found by Horst[25] in *Polygonum persecaria,* by Weiss[26] in *Trifolium repens, Acacia, Gambircatechu,* flowers of *Crataegus,* and leaves of *Myrtus checken;* by Loewe[27] in *Catechu;* by Hummel[28] in the leaves of *Cherianthus cheri;* by Pilgrim[29] in the coloring matter of *Delphinium zali;* and by Perkin and Wood[30] in the leaves

[7] Ann., 37, p. 101; Monatsh, 5, p. 72.
[8] Am. Jr. Pharm., 51, p. 118.
[9] C. Neubaur, Versuchsst, 16, p. 427.
[10] Jr. Chem. Soc., 71, p. 1131.
[11] Jr. Chem. Soc., 73, p. 697.
[12] Ann., 82, p. 197; Apoth. Zeit., (1901 p. 351.
[13] Jr. Chem. Soc., 67, p. 30.
[14] Jr. Chem. Soc., 71, p. 1131.
[15] Proc. Chem. Soc., 16, p. 295.
[16] Am. Jr. Pharm., 64, p. 295.
[17] Proc. Chem. Soc., 15, p. 179.
[18] Bull. Soc. Chim., 28, p. 337.
[19] Wien. Acad. Ber., 33, p. 565.
[20] Jr. Chem. Soc., 69, p 1295.
[21] Jr. Chem. Soc., 81, p. 477.
[22] Jr. Chem. Soc., 95, p. 2181.
[23] Proc. Chem. Soc., 19, p. 284; Jr. Chem. Soc., 49, p. 1295, 1556.
[24] Jr. Chem. Soc., 71, p. 1194.
[25] Chem. Ztg., 25, p. 2055.
[26] Arch. Pharm., (3) 26, p. 665.
[27] Zeit. f. Anal. Chem., 12, p. 127.
[28] Jr. Chem. Soc., 69, p. 1568.
[29] Jr. Chem. Soc., 73, p. 273.
[30] Jr. Chem. Soc., 73, p. 381.

of *Ailanthus glandulosa,* also in the leaves of *Rhus rhodanthema.*[81]

Pure quercetin presents the appearance of a lemon yellow crystalline powder made up of tiny needle like crystals. It is almost insoluble in cold water, soluble in alcohol, very difficultly soluble in ether, and easily soluble in dilute alkalies. It crystallizes with three molecules of water of crystallization which it loses at 130°. In alcoholic solution it gives a dark green coloration with ferric chloride which turns black upon heating. With lead acetate it gives a red precipitate. It reduces silver solutions when cold and Fehling's solution when heated. Quercetin melts at 250°. When treated with chromic acid and acetic acid it is oxidized to quercetone.

To fabrics mordanted with aluminum quercetin imparts a brownish yellow color; with chromium, a deep orange color; with iron, a dark olive; and with tin, a bright orange yellow.

Quercetone.

O
C   CH   COH
HOC   C — O — C — C   COH
                 ‖
HC   C — C — COH   CH   CH
           ‖
           O
C
O

Quercetone,[82] the oxidation product of quercetin, crystallizes in small deep red needle like crystals which melt above 360°. It dissolves in alkalies with a blue, and in concentrated sulphuric acid with a red coloration. When heated with acetic acid and zinc dust acetylated hydroxy quercetin is obtained as a colorless, amorphous powder which yields upon hydrolysis penthydroxy-1, 3, 4, 3′, 4′-flavonol. This crystallizes in small yellow needles which lose a molecule of water at 160°, and melt at 352°–355°. Both alkaline hydroxides and sulphuric acid dissolve it with a yellow color. Pentmethoxy flavonol forms small colorless crystals which melt at 147°–149°.

---

[81] Jr. Chem. Soc., 73, p. 1017.
[82] Ber., 44, p. 3487.

Literature on Quercetin.

Bartolloti, — Gazz. chim. ital., 24, II. p. 480.

Bolley, — Ann., 37, p. 101; 125, p. 54.

Bolley and Mylius, — Schweitzerische Poly. Zeit., 9, p. 22.

Bolley, — Jahresber d. Chem., 1861, p. 709.

Chevreul, — Lecons de Chem. app. a la Teinture.

Dunstan and Henry, — Jr. Chem. Soc., 73, p. 219.

Foerster, — Ber., 15, p. 214.

Gintl, — Jahresber. d. Chem., 1868, p. 801.

Herzig, — C. r., 5, p. 72; 6, p. 863; 9, pp. 537 and 548; 10, p. 561; 12, p. 172; 14, pp. 39 and 53; 15, p. 683; 16, p. 312; 17, p. 421; 18, p. 700.

Herzig, — Monatsh., 6, p. 863; 9, p. 541; 15, p. 696.

Hlasiwetz, — C. r., 29, p. 10.

Hlasiwetz, — Ann., 96, p. 123.

Hlasiwetz, — Jahresber. d. Chem., 1864, p. 564; 1867, p. 732.

Kostanecki, — Ber., 37, p. 793, 1402.

Liebermann, — C. r., 16, p. 180.

Liebermann and Hamburger, — B., 12, p. 1179.

Liebermann and Hoerman, — Ann., 196, p. 299, 338.

Loewe, — Zeit. f. analyt. Chem., 12, p. 127, 233.

Lushing, — Dingler's Poly. Jr., 139, p. 1319.

Mandeline, — Pharm. Ztg. f. Russ., 22, p. 329.

Niernstein and Wheldale, — B., 44, p. 3487.

Perkin, — Jr. Chem. Soc., 67, p. 644; 69, p. 1295; 71, p. 1131, 1135, 1191; 73, p. 231, 267, 381, 1017, 1135; 74, p. 278; 75, p. 837; 77, p. 426; 81, p. 477; 85, p. 56; 95, p. 1855, 2181.

Rigaud,— Ann., 90, p. 283.

Roechleder, — C. r., 33, p. 365.

Roechleder, — Jahresber. d. Chem., 1859, p. 523; 1866, p. 654; 1867, p. 731.

Rudolph, — Pharm. Post., 26, p. 529.

Schuetzenberger and Paraf, — Zeit. f. Chem., 1826, p. 41.

Schunck, — Chem. Gazette., 399, p. 20.

Stein, — Zeit. f. prakt. Chem., 1863, p. 467.

Stein, — Jr. f. prakt. Chem., 58, 399; 85, p. 351; 88, p. 280; 89, p. 491.

Wagner, — Chem. Centrlbl., 1873, p. 586.

Zwenger and Dronke, — Ann., (Suppl. I.) p. 257.

Rhamnetin,—Quercetin-3-monomethyl ether, or Trihydroxy-1, 3′, 4′-methoxy -3-flavonol.

CH CH COH
CH_3OC C — O — C — C COH
COH
HC C — C — COH CH CH
O
COH

Rhametin was known as early as 1841 in the form of glucoside then called rhamnin[1] but now known as xanthorhamnin. It was hydrolized in 1858 by Gellatly,[2] and the sugar was identified as rhamnose by Berend[3] in 1878. Later Tanret[4] found that xanthorhamnin was a mixed glucoside containing two molecules of rhamnose and one of galactose. The constitution[5] of rhamnetin and other methyl ethers of quercetin has been the subject of considerable chemical study, the question under consideration being the position of the methoxy groups. Perkin,[6] in 1902 showed that by careful decomposition with alkalies the monomethyl ether of phloroglucin is obtained and that the methoxy group must therefore be in that part of the molecule from which the phloroglucinol is obtained. The formula for rhamnetin according to Perkin is given above.

According to Czapek, rhamnetin occurs as the glucoside in the fruit and in the bark of several species of *Rhamnus.* Kane,[7] Gellatly,[8] Schuetzenberger,[9] and Liebermann[10] find it in the "Gelbeern" or "Avignonkoerner," the fruit of *Rhamnus infectoria* and *R. tinctoria.*

Rhamnetin crystallizes best from phenol, in which it is easily soluble when heated. It separates on cooling in small bright lemon yellow crystals. It is sparingly soluble in warm water and very slightly soluble in the ordinary organic solvents. It

---

[1] Jr. Chem. Soc., 27, p. 666.
[2] Chem. Centrlbl., 29, p. 477.
[3] Ber., 9, p. 1853.
[4] C. r., 129, p. 725; Bull. Soc. Chim., (3) 21, p. 1073.
[5] Monats., 4, p. 889; 9, p. 548; 10, p. 561.
[6] Jr. Chem. Soc., 81, p. 569.
[7] Berz. Jahresb. 24, 505.
[8] Jahresb., 1838, p. 474.
[9] Jahresb., 1868. p. 774.
[10] Ann., 196, p. 312.

dissolves readily in alkalies with a yellow color. In alcoholic solutions it yields a brownish green color with ferric chloride, an orange yellow color with lead acetate and a reddish brown precipitate with lime or baryta water. It reduces an ammonical silver solution in the cold, Fehling's solution when warmed.

Isorhamnetin,—Quercetin-3'-monomethyl ether, or Trihydroxy-1, 3, 4'-methoxy-3'-flavonol.

```
          CH                              CH     COCH3
    HOC        C—O— C — C                          COH
                    ||
    HC         C—C —COH                   CH  CH
            C     ||
            OH    O
```

Isorhamnetin was first isolated by Perkin and Hummel[1] in 1896, from the petals of the yellow wallflower, *Cherianthus cheri,* and later by Perkin and Pilgrim[2] from the flowers of*Delphinium zali.* Because by oxidation in alkaline solution isorhamnetin yields vanillic acid, Perkin[3] concludes that it has the methoxy group in position -3'- as given above.

Isorhamnetin occurs, as stated above, in the flowers of *Cherianthus cheri* and of *Delphinium zali,* along with quercetin. It crystallizes in masses of fine, brilliant yellow, needle like crystals which are difficultly soluble in boiling alcohol and in acetic acid. With lead acetate it gives an orange red preciptate, with ferric chloride a greenish black coloration. Fused with alkalies it yields protocatechuic acid and phloroglucin.

Rhamnazin,—Quercetin-3, 3'-dimethyl ether, or Dihydroxy-1, 4'-dimethoxy 3, 3'-flavonol.

Rhamnazin was first found by Perkin[1] in "Persian berries," the fruit of various species of *Rhamnus,* while trying to purify rhamnetin, in 1895, and shown by him to be dimethyl-3, 3'-quercetin, as below.

[1] Jr. Chem. Soc., 69, p. 1566.
[2] Jr. Chem. Soc., 73, p. 267.
[3] Proc. Chem. Soc., 14, p. 56.
[1] Jr. Chem. Soc., 67, p. 496; 71, p. 819.

```
         CH                              CH ___ COCH₃
CH₃O/        \C — O — C — C/           \COH
                          ||
HC  \        /C — C — COH                CH  CH
                  ||
         C        O
         |
         OH
```

Rhamnazin occurs in the fruit of *Rhamnus infectoria,*[1] and perhaps in other species of *Rhamnus.* Pure rhamnazin forms yellow needle like crystals which melt at 214°–215° and somewhat resemble anthraquinone in appearance. They are less soluble in acetic acid than are those of quercetin and very slightly soluble in alcohol. From acetic acid rhamnazin crystallizes with one molucule of water of crystallization which it loses at 100°. It dissolves easily in alkalies with an orange red color, with lime or baryta water it gives an insoluble orange red precipitate. The alcohol solution gives an olive green coloration with ferric chloride. It forms a triacetyl, also a trobenzoyl derivative.

Morin,—Penthydroxy- 1, 3, 2′, 4′, α-flavone, or Tetrahydroxy- 1, 3, 2′, 4′ -flavonol.

```
         CH                              COH   CH
HOC/         \C — O — C — C/             \COH
                          ||
HC  \        /C — C — COH                CH  CH
                  ||
         C        O
         |
         OH
```

Morin was first found by Chevreul[1] in yellow wood, *Morus tinctoria,* in 1830, and later by Perkin and Cope[2] in the Indian dye stuff *Artocarpus tinctoria.* It closely resembles quercetin in appearance and reactions. Perkin[3] in his work on morin in 1896 assigned to it the constitutional formula of quercetin with the catechol nucleus replaced by a resorcinol group. This formula was verified by the work of Kostanecki[4] in 1904, and further

[1] Jr., Chim. Med., 6, p. 158.
[2] Jr. Chem. Soc., 67, p. 937.
[3] Jr. Chem. Soc., 69, p. 792; Chem. News., 78, p. 253.
[4] Ber., 37, p. 2350.

confirmed by his final synthesis[5] of morin from hydroxy-2′-tetramethoxy-4, 5, 2′, 4′ -chalkon in 1906.

Morin occurs in fustic wood, ***Morus tinctoria***,[1] the wood of *Chlorophora tinctoria*,[6] and of *Artocarpus integrifolia*,[2] and *Maclura tinctoria*.[6]

Morin crystallizes in long needle like crystals which are very slightly soluble in water, easily soluble in alcohol and less easily soluble in ether. It is not at all soluble in carbon disulphide, but soluble in alkalies with a yellow color. In alcoholic solutions it gives an olive green color with ferric chloride. It reduces an ammoniacal silver solution in the cold, Fehling's solution when warm. Treated with potassium salts a yellow precipitate is obtained which corresponds to the formula $C_{15}H_9O_7K$. With sodium acetate the corresponding sodium salt is obtained. Fused with alkalies morin yields phloroglucine and β-resorcylic acid. To wools mordanted with aluminum morin imparts a yellowish olive color; with chromium, a deep brown; with tin, a bright yellow; and with iron, a dark olive brown color.

Besides those mentioned above, morin has been prepared and studied by the following chemists:

Wagner, — Jr. f. prakt. Chem., 50, p. 182.
Hlasiwetz and Pfaundler, — Ann., 127, p. 351.
Loewe, — Zeit, anal. Chem., 14, p. 119.
Benedikt, — B., 8, p. 606.
Benedikt and Hazura, — Monatsh., 5, p. 167.
Perkin, — Jr. Chem. Soc. 67, p. 649; 69, p. 792; 75, p. 433.
Herzig, — Monatsh., 18, p. 702.

Hexhydroxy flavones.

Myricetin,—Hexhydroxy-1, 3, 3′, 4′, 5′, a-flavone, or, Penthydroxy-1, 3, 3′, 4′, 5′ -flavonol.

Myricetin was first isolated by Perkin,[1] in 1896, from ***Myrica nagi***, an Indian dye stuff, and named by him from its source.

---

[5] Ber., 39, p. 81; 95, 627.

It was later isolated, by Perkin[4] and his associates, from a number of other dye stuffs and has been found to be a hydroxy quercetin.

Myricetin occurs as the glucoside myricitrin in the bark of *Myrica nagi*,[1] and *M. gale*.[2] In the leaves of *Rhus coriaria*,[2] *R. cotinus*,[2] and *R. metopium*.[2] It also occurs in *Pistachia lentiscus*,[2] *Haematoxylon campechianum*,[2] and in the leaves of *Arctostaphylos uva ursi*.[2]

Myricetin crystallizes in small clear yellow crystals which melt with decomposition above 300°. It dissolves with difficulty in boiling water, more easily in alcohol, and almost not at all in chloroform and acetic acid. It dissolves in potassium hydroxide solution with a yellow color which changes in the air to bluish, and becomes finally dull violet red in color. Concentrated alkali solutions give a permanent red color which goes through all the above changes upon dilution. Ammonia gives a more reddish color, lead acetate, a reddish orange color which becomes yellow upon boiling. Myricetin is dissolved with a red color in sulphuric acid and is precipitated upon the addition of water. Ferric chloride gives a black color in alcoholic solutions. Fused with alkalies myricetin rapidly becomes brown and yields principally gallic acid and phloroglucin. Myricetin dyes fabrics mordanted with aluminum a brownish orange; with chromium, a red brown; with tin, a deep orange red; and with iron, an olive black.

Gossypetin.

In 1899 Perkin[1] isolated from the yellow flowers of the Indian Cotton—*Gossypium herbaceum* a yellow pigment which he called gossypetin. This substance has the molecular composition $C_{15}H_{10}O_8$. It is isomeric with myricetin with six hydroxy groups, two of which are in relatively ortho-position. In its behavior it closely resembles the flavone derivatives. It is probably a member of the flavone group.

Gossypetin occurs principally in the form of the glucoside gossypitrin in the flowers of *Gossypium herbaceum*,[1] the Indian

---

[4] Czapek, p. 521.
[1] Jr. Chem. Soc., 69, p. 1287.
[2] Jr. Chem. Soc., 81, p. 203; 77, p. 424, 427.
[1] Jr. Chem. Soc., 75, p. 825.
[2] Jr. Chem. Soc., 95, p. 1855.

cotton, and in the flowers of *Hibiscus sabdariffa.*[2] The Indian cotton flowers are used by the natives as a dye stuff. The seeds of the plant also contain a somewhat feeble yellow dyestuff, not identical with gossypetin, which by the action of acid is converted into the so called cotton seed blue.[3] Moreover, in the bark of the stem there exists a dye[4] which somewhat resembles gossypetin.

Gossypetin crystallizes in glistening yellow needles. Its hexacetyl derivative melts at 222°–224°. Treated with sulphuric acid in acetic acid solution it forms a gossypetin sulphate consisting of glistening orange-red needles. This compound is decomposed by water into gossypetin and sulphuric acid. The hydrochloride prepared in the same way forms orange crystals and is very unstable. The hydriodide which forms orange red crystals is more stable. The hydrochloride could not be analyzed but the others are evidently formed by addition of one molecule of the acid to one of the pigment. This behavior suggests the oxonium formation.

Gossypetin is very soluble in alcohol and slightly soluble in water. It dissolves in alkalies with an orange red color. Fused with alkalies it yields phloroglucin and protocatechuic acid. To wools mordanted with aluminum it gives a pale orange brown color; with tin, an orange red color, with chromium, a dull brown and with iron a deep dull olive color.

The dyeing properties of the flowers of the Indian cotton are very distinct from those of gossypetin, due to the fact that they contain the glucoside and not the free coloring matter. With the ordinary mordants the following shades are obtained: aluminum, dull yellow; tin, orange, brown; chromium, dull brown-yellow; iron, dull olive.

I. B. 2.) *Butein.*

While not a flavone derivative, butein is nevertheless referable to the same hydrocarbons as the flavone derivatives, being a tetrahydroxy-4, 5, 3′, 4′-diphenyl-1-3-propene-1-one-3, or tetrahy droxy chalkon.

[2] C. r., 53, p. 444; Anzeiger der Akademie der Weissenschaften in Krakow, Nov. 1897.

```
HOC_____COH                              CH  CH
   /     \                  O           /    \
HC<       >C—CH==CH—C—C<        >COH
   \     /                             \    /
  CH   CH                             CH   COH
```

Butein[1] occurs either as such or in glucosidal formation, in the form of butin, in the flowers of ***Butea frondosa.*** Its synthesis from dimethylprotocatechuic aldehyde and monomethyl resacetophenone as well as its formation from butin[2] have been discussed in a previous chapter.

Butein crystallizes in needle like crystals which melt at 213°–215°. It is readily soluble in alcohol, somewhat soluble in ether, more sparingly soluble than butin in hot water. It dissolves in alkaline solutions with a deep orange red color. In alcoholic solutions with lead acetate it gives a deep red precipitate, with ferric chloride an olive brown coloration. In cold sulphuric acid it dissolves with an orange color, upon the addition of water the butein is precipitated unchanged.

Butein dyes wools mordanted with aluminum a beautiful orange color, with chromium a deep terra cotta, with tin a beautiful yellow, and with iron a brownish olive.

I. B. 3.) *The anthocyanin pigments.*

The so called anthocyanin pigments have long attracted the attention of both chemists and botanists, and have called forth considerable work from both classes of investigators. From time to time colored substances have been extracted from plant organs supposed to be colored by anthocyanin pigments and have been made the subject of special investigation. These colored substances, though sometimes crystalline, were probably seldom pure, so that little chemical knowledge was gained either of the special pigment studied or of the anthocyanins as a class. In addition to the above, many theories, all of which have been more or less unsatisfactory, have been advanced to account for both the appearance and the disappearance of color in flowers, fruits, and autumn foliage.

The recent exhaustive study, by Willstaetter, of anthocyanin

[1] Proc. Chem. Soc., 10, p. 11; 19, p. 133; 85, p. 1495.
[2] See Butin, Formula of saturation C_nH_{2n-14}.

pigments in some plants, while not satisfactory in every detail, is a long step in advance. This work not only explains much concerning the chemistry of the anthocyanin pigments that has hitherto been unexplained; but it places the anthocyanins in a class, and shows the close chemical relationship between the various anthocyanin pigments studied, and also between the anthocyanins and other pigments occurring with them in the plant.

Anthocyanins are red, blue and purple pigments extracted from flowers, fruits, and leaves by water and dilute alcohol. They are insoluble in ether, are turned red by acids, blue or green by alkalies, and give green, green-blue, gray-green, or yellow precipitates with lead acetate. It is commonly supposed that the purple color of flowers and fruits is due to the free pigment, the blue color to an alkaline combination, and the red color to an acid combination of the pigment.

The anthocyanins, according to Willstaetter, are present in the plants only as glucosides, sometimes as mono- and sometimes as diglucosides. The sugar molecule with which the pigment is combined is generally that of glucose, though in at least one instance galactose is present. The anthocyanins all exhibit a characteristic reaction, the anthocyanidin reaction. An anthocyanin dissolved in a normal or twice normal solution of sulphuric acid is unaffected by shaking with amyl alcohol. After hydrolysis, however, the colorod anthocyanidin is quantitatively extracted by the amyl alcohol, forming a reddish violet solution which slowly, more rapidly in the presence of sodium acetate, changes to a bluish violet.

All of the anthocyanins so far studied are very closely related, the color bases of the various glucosides being hydroxy and methoxy derivatives of pelargonidin, the least highly oxygenated of the known anthocyanins. They are also closely related to the flavone derivatives, so many of which constitute the yellow plant pigments, and many of which occur side by side with the anthocyanin pigments in the plants. According to Willstaetter the free anthocyanin pigments are isomers of some of the flavone pigments, the isomerism between them existing, not in the position of substitution in one or the other of the two benzene nuclei, but in the transformation, by the changing of valence of the ether oxygen from two to four, of the pyron to a pyrylium grouping, and of a difference in the position of the hydroxyl group in the pyrylium cycle, all of the anthocyanin pigments so far known possessing a hydroxyl group in the flavonol position. For example, luteolin and cyanidin are both represented by the formula $C_{15}H_{10}O_6$.

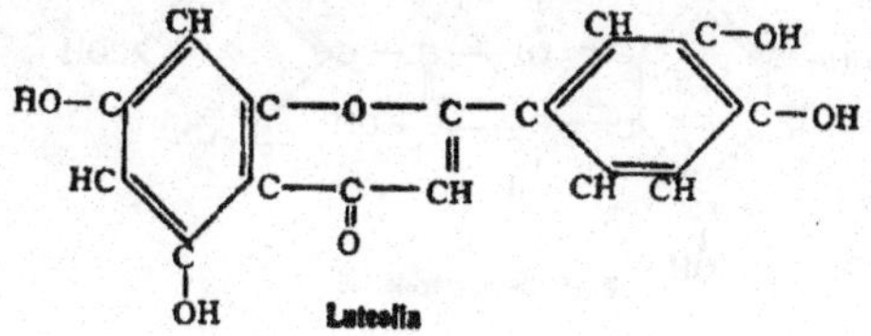

Luteolin

The formula for free cyanidin is not known.

The hydrochloride of luteolin Willstaetter represents by formula I, and that of cyanidin by formula II. below.

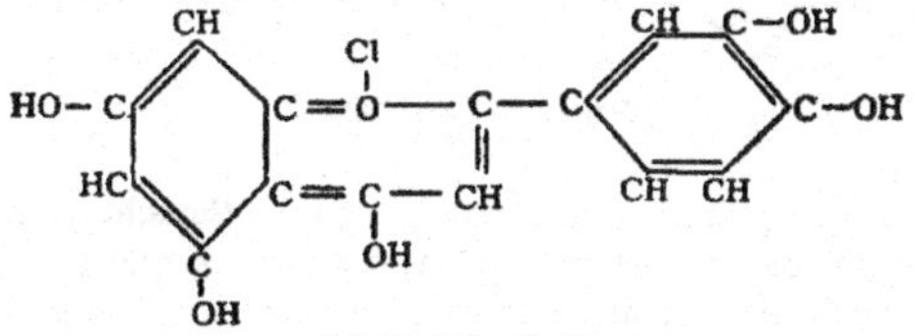

Luteolin hydrochloride

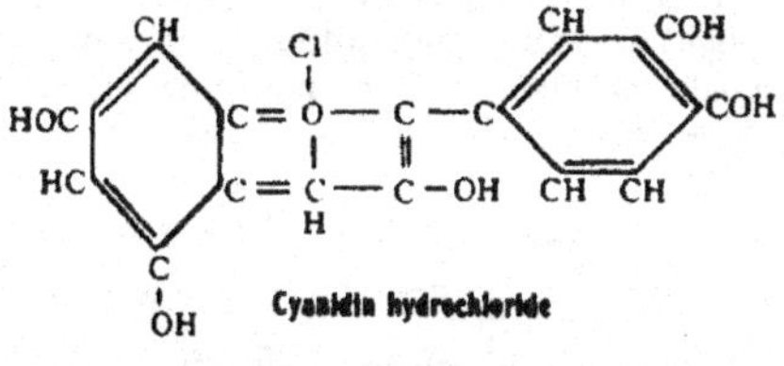

Cyanidin hydrochloride

While this difference of position of a hydroxy group may be sufficient to explain the difference in properties of the two groups of pigments in acid combination, something more seems to be required to explain this difference in the acid free form, since many of the flavone pigments as well as the anthocyanin pigments are flavonols. Moreover it does not appear to be sufficient to explain the difference between such isomers as, for example, delphinidin hydrochloride and quercetin hydrochloride, quercetin having an hydroxy group in the flavonol position.

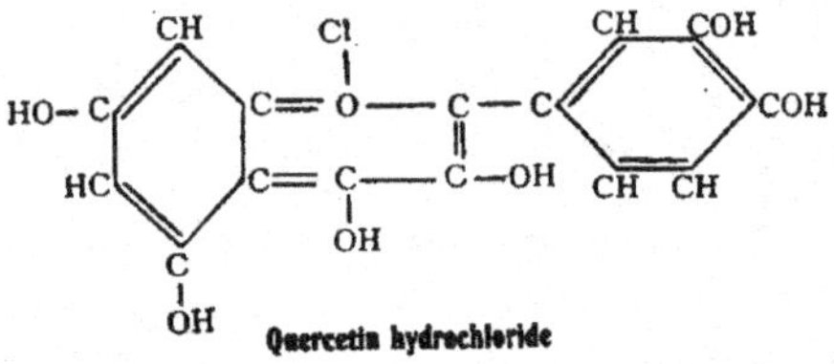

Quercetin hydrochloride

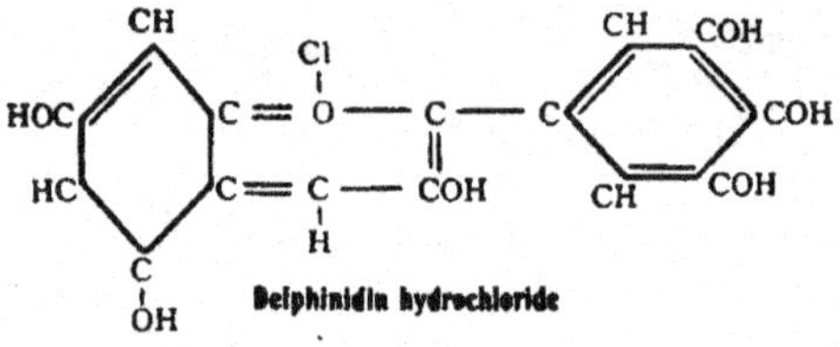

Delphinidin hydrochloride

The anthocyanin pigments have long been thought of as being of a quinoidal character. This supposition was encouraged by the oxidation of quercetin and chrysin, by Niernstein and Wheldale,[1] to quercetone and chrysone respectively, these oxidation products being "anthocyanin like." Willstaetter and Everest[2] sought to explain the constitution of cyanin by assuming a quinoidal arrangement and classifying the anthocyanins as paraquinoidal flavone derivatives, as below:

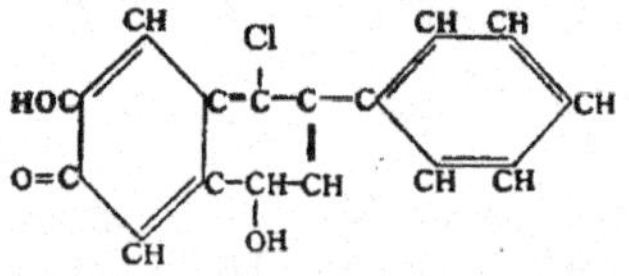

From such a molecule one would expect a hydroxy hydroquinone as one of the products of abbau. Since no such product, but phloroglucine just as with the majority of flavone

[1] Ber., 44, p. 3487; 45, p. 499.
[2] Ann., 408, p. 18.

pigments, is obtained, the quinoidal configuration as a possible explanation was abandoned and the arrangement of double bonds of the pyrylium grouping adopted instead. Whether or not the difficulties in the way of accepting Willstaetter's furmula are more easily explained away than are those in the way of accepting the quinoidal formula is still a matter of opinion.

Among the anthocyanins thus far studied pelargonidin is isomeric with apiginin and galangin. Cyanidin is isomeric with luteolin, lotoflavin, fisetin, and kaempherol. Paeonidin, a methyl ether of cyanidin is isomeric with kaempherid, a methyl ether of kaempherol. Delphinidin is isomeric with quercetin and morin, while myrtillidin, a methyl ether of delphinidin is isomeric with rhamnetin and isorhamnetin, both methyl ethers of quercetin, and malvinidin and oenidin, dimethyl ethers of delphinidin are isomeric with rhamnazin, a dimethyl ether of quercetin.

The isomerism of the above named compounds is probably not to be doubted. That this isomerism consists only in the different position of a hydroxyl group in the pyrylium ring, even in acid combination, is open to question, since no such marked difference in properties exists between the flavonols and the true flavones as is found to exist between the flavone derivatives and the anthocyanins.

None of the neutral pigments, isomeric with the flavone pigments appear to have been isolated as such. They have been obtained as oxonium salts formed by the addition of a molecule of acid to a molecule of the pigment, as the colorless pseudo base, obtained by the elimination of the elements of hydrochloric acid and the addition of the elements of a molecule of water, and as the color base, a colored modification of the pseudo base into which it changes upon standing in concentrated solution.

According to Willstaetter red and pink colors in the organs examined are due to acid compounds of the pigment, oxonium salts; purple and violet colors to the free pigments; and blue colors to metallic derivatives of the pigment. The blue cornflower is probably colored by the potassium salt of the cyanin, and the scarlet geranium by the compound of pelargonin with tartaric acid, while the purple delphinum is supposed to be colored by the neutral delpninin.

Tetrahydroxides.

Pelargonidin.

According to Willstaetter pelargonidin chloride, the oxonium salt of pelargonidin, is probably represented by formula I. given below, though he also recognizes the possibility of its being represented by formula II. Willstaetter prefers the first fomula because he regards the second as the structural formula of a flavone derivative.

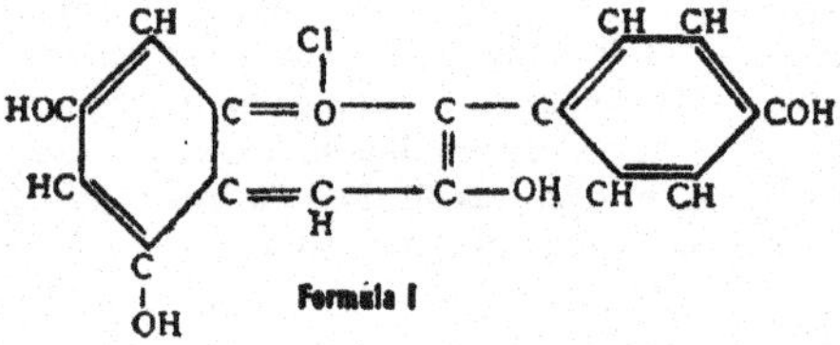

Formula I

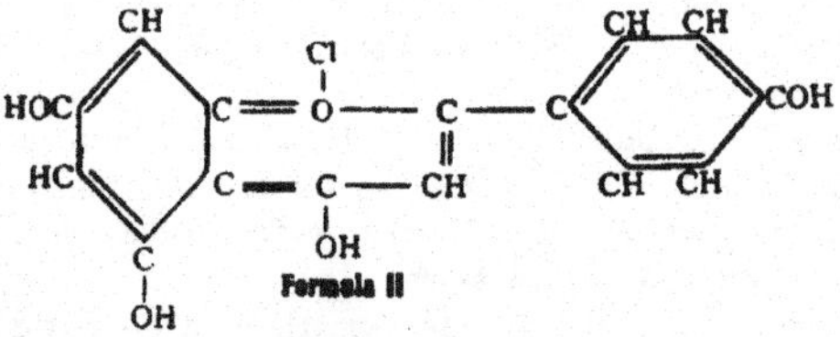

Formula II

Pelargonidin exists in the blossoms of the red geranium, *Pelargonium zonale,* combined with two molecules of glucose as the glucoside pelargonin.

The geranium pigment was isolated by Griffiths[1] from the blossoms of the red geranium in 1903. Griffiths decided that the pigment has the formula $C_{15}H_{10}O_6$ and that it forms a red diacetyl derivative.

In 1908 Wenzell[2] again isolated the crystalline red pigment from the flowers of *Pelargonium zonale,* but he made no chemical study of the compound.

During the winter of 1911–1912 the writer, having access to large quantities of geranium blossoms, again isolated the red crystalline pigment. The substance crystallized in fine needle

[1] Ber., 36, p. 3956.

[2] Pacific Pharmacist, 1908, p. 446.

shaped crystals of a high melting point and a bright red color. The crystals dried in masses of a brownish color with a beautiful green reflection. This substance was no glucoside. If it existed as such in the plant, it was hydrolized in the process of preparation by the sulphuric acid used to decompose the lead precipitate. The crystalline substance was insoluble in ether, chloroform, hydrocarbon oils, and carbon disulphide, almost insoluble in hot water and in 95 per cent alcohol, but easily soluble in 60–70 per cent alcohol when heated. It was possibly the pelargonidin sulphate described by Willstaetter.

This compound gave a yellow acetyl derivative when heated with acetic acid anhydride and anhydrous sodium acetate. This acetyl derivative, computed upon Griffith's formula of $C_{15}H_{10}O_6$, contained five acetyl groups. This, interpreted in the light of Willstaetter's formula would probably mean that the sulphate, in the process of acetylization, was changed to the acetate and that all four of the hydroxy groups were acetylized. When heated in alcoholic solution with zinc and acetic acid the red color of the crystalline pigment disappeared leaving a colorless solution. This, after standing exposed to the air, gradually became deep red in color. No crystals could be induced to separate from this red solution.

Willstaetter criticises severely the old method of attempting to separate anthocyanin pigments by precipitation with lead acetate. However just this criticism may be when applied to anthocyanins in general the writer will not venture to say. The above described pigment, however, was easily obtained, apparently in a pure condition, by precipitating an aqueous extract of fresh geranium blossoms with lead acetate and decomposing the precipitate with sulphuric acid. The exact details of the process need not be given here.

In 1911 Grafe[3] isolated what he considered as two pigments from the scarlet geranium, one glucosidal and the other not glucosidal in character. Willstaetter says that as a matter of fact both of Grafe's pigments are glucosides, and that only one is present in the plant, the second being a mixture of the pigment with other substances.

Willstaetter's pelargonidin was separated in the form of the oxonium salt of the glucoside pelargonin. This upon hydroly-

[3] Sitzungsber. d. Wien Akad. Wiss. math. nat. kl., 120, p. 765.

sis yields pelargonidin chloride which crystallizes in three different forms. The sulphate crystallizes in needles.

Willstaetter's idea of the structure of pelargonidin is obtained from its abbau with 50 per cent potassium hydroxide solution when phloroglucin, p-hydroxybenzoic acid, and small quantities of protocatechuic acid are obtained. It is isomeric with apiginin and galangin.

Willstaetter found pelargonin in the scarlet flowers of *Pelargonium zonale,*[4] also in the scarlet red varieties of dahlia,[5] known as "*Rakete*" and "*Alt Heidelberg,*" also in a violet red variety of dahlia.

Penthydroxides.

Cyanidin.

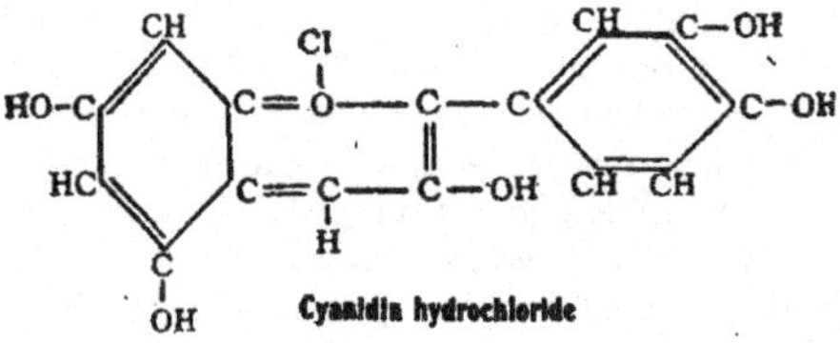

Cyanidin hydrochloride

The above formula represents the constitution of cyanidin hydrochloride according to Willstaetter's more favored formula.

As early as 1854 Fremy and Cloez[1] isolated a blue pigment from the cornflower which they called cyanin. According to these investigators there are three kinds of pigments in plants, the green, called chlorophyll, the yellow known as xanthine and xantheine, and the red and blue, which they called cyanin. The red and rose colored flowers owe their color to the cyanin colored by acids in the juice of the plant.

In 1913 Willstaetter and Everest[2] again isolated the blue pigment from cornflowers and made it the subject of an exhaustive investigation. They found that cyanin, the pigment, is a glucoside which they obtained as the hydrochloride. Upon hydrolysis this glucoside gave cyanidin chloride. To the hydro-

[4] Ann., 408, p. 42.
[5] Ann., 408, p. 151.
[1] Jr. de Pharm., 58, p. 249.
[2] Ann., 401, p. 189.

chloride of the glucoside they assigned the formula $C_{28}H_{33}O_{17}Cl.3H_2O$, to that of the cyanidin $C_{16}H_{13}O_7Cl$. As the result of a later determination these formulae were changed to $C_{27}H_{31}O_{16}Cl.2\frac{1}{2}H_2O$ and $C_{15}H_{11}O_6Cl$. respectively, with the structural formula as given above.

Cyanidin exists as the glucoside cyanin in *Centauria cyanus*, the corn flower, in the dark red varieties of the cactus dahlia[4] known as "J. H. Jackson," "Harold," "Matchless," "Othello," and "Night," in the petals of *Rosa gallica*, and in the fruit of the whortleberry, *Vaccinium vitis idaea*, as the glucoside idaein, a compound of one molecule of cyanidin with one of galactose. Cyanidin is isomeric with lotoflavin, luteolin, fisetin, and kaempherol.

Paeonidin,—a monomethyl ether of cyanin.

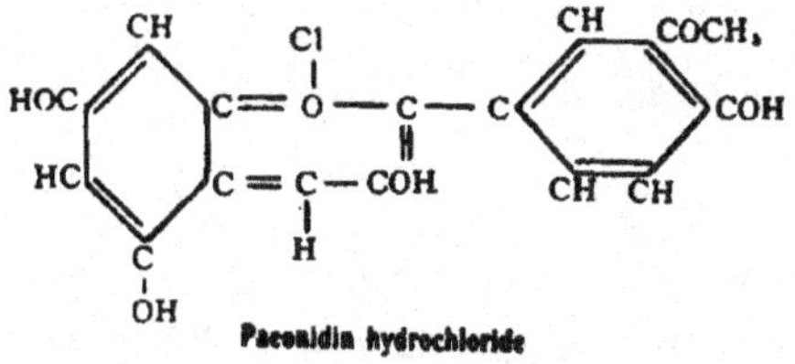

Paeonidin hydrochloride

Paeonidin[1] exists in the paeony blossoms as the glucoside paeonin, a compound of paeonidin with two molecules of glucose. Treated with hydriodic acid it yields cyanin and methyl iodide. The formula for paeonidin hydrochloride favored by Willstaetter is given above. Paeonidin is isomeric with luteolin methyl ether and kaempherid.

Hexhydroxides.

Delphinidin.

Delphinidin[1] occurs as the glucoside delphinin in the blossoms of *Delphinium consolida* where it exists along with the isomeric

---

[3] Ann., 408, p. 1.
[4] Ann., 408, p. 151.
[1] Ann., 408, p. 186.
[1] Ann., 408, p. 61.

quercetin and the closely related kaempherol.[3] The glucoside delphinin is a compound of one molecule of delphinidin with two of glucose.

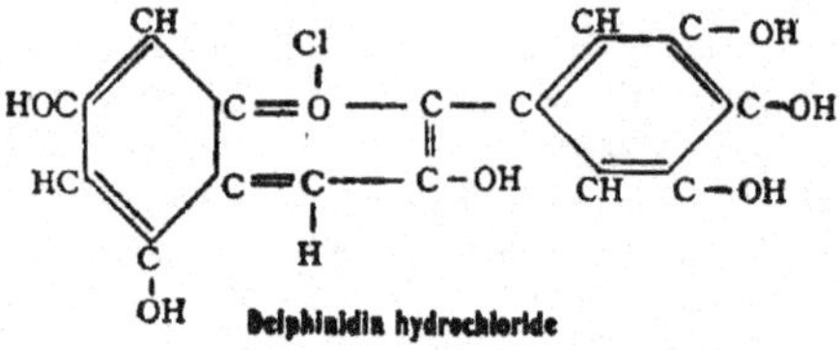

Delphinidin hydrochloride

Delphinidin is isomeric with quercetin and morin. The structural formula most favored by Willstaetter is given above.

Myrtillidin,—a monomethyl ether of delphinidin.

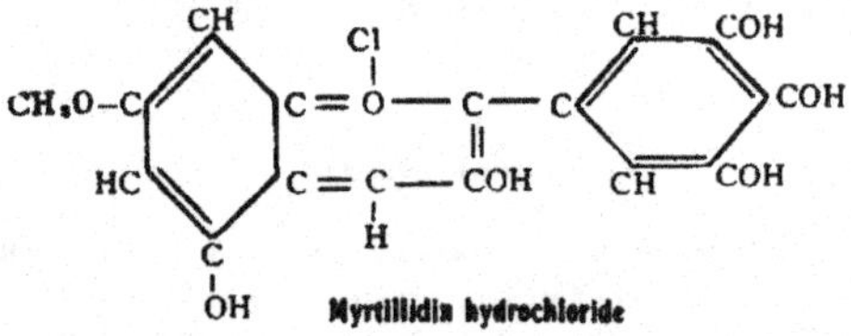

Myrtillidin hydrochloride

Myrtillidin was found by Willstaetter to exist in the form of the glucoside myrtillin in combination with one molecule of glucose in the fruit of the bilberry, *Vaccinium myrtillus;*[1] also as the glucoside althaein in the blossoms of *Althaea rosea,*[2] the wild mallow. Myrtillidin is isomeric with rhamnetin and isorhamnetin, monomethyl ethers of quercetin.

---

[3] Jr. Chem. Soc., 73, p. 275; 81, p. 585.
[1] Ann., 408, p. 103.
[2] Ann., 408, p. 110.

Oenidin,—a dimethyl ether of delphinidin.

```
          CH           Cl            CH   COH
        /    \         |            /   \
CH₃O—C        C = O — C — C        C      COCH₃
     |        |            ‖
    HC        C = C — COH          CH   COH
        \    /      |
          C         H
          |
          OH
```

The pigment from grapes had been separated in a more or less impure state many times before Willstaetter undertook his study of anthocyanin pigments. Mulder,[1] in 1856 obtained the pigment in the form of a bluish black mass, Mawmene,[2] in 1856, obtained the same substance and named it "oenocyanin." In 1858 Glenard obtained the pigment as an amorphous substance which he called "oenolin" and to which he assigned the formula $C_{20}H_{20}O_{10}$. Gautier[4] made several investigations of the coloring matter of grapes, continuing his studies for a number of years. Gautier traced a close relationship between the grape pigment and the tannins. Willstaetter,[5] in 1915, found the pigment to exist in the form of the glucoside oenin in *Vitis vinifera.* To the product of hydrolysis he gave the formula above.

Oenidin is an isomer of rhamnazin, a dimethyl ether of quercetin.

Malvinidin,—a dimethyl ether of delphinidin.

```
        CH          Cl           CH   COH
       /   \        |           /   \
 HOC        C = O — C — C             COCH₃
    |       |           ‖
  HC        C — C — COH          CH   COH
       \   /        |
        C           H
        |
        OCH₃
```

¹ Die Chemie des Wines, 44, p. 228.
² Le Travail des Vins.
³ C. r., 47, p. 268; Ann. Chim. Phys., (3) 54, p. 366.
⁴ C. r., 86., p. 1507; 87, p. 64; 114, p. 623.
⁵ Ann. 408, p. 87.

Malvinidin was found by Willstaetter to exist in the violet flowers of the wild mallow, or wood mallow, ***Malva sylvestris,*** where it occurs in combination with two molecules of glucose as the diglucoside malvin. Malvinidin is isomeric with oenidin, also with rhamnazin, a dimethyl ether of quercetin.

II. PIGMENTS REFERABLE TO DIHYDROANTHRACENE AND HOMOLOGUES.

A. Pigments referable to dihydroanthracene.

B. Pigments referable to homologues of dihydroanthracene.

   1. Pigments referable to methyl -1- dihydroanthracene.
   2. Pigments referable to methyl -2- dihydroanthracene.

Most if not all of the plant pigments referable to dihydroanthacene and its homologues, are derivatives of anthraquinone and its homologues, the quinones being tetrahydroxy derivatives of the underlying hydrocarbons.

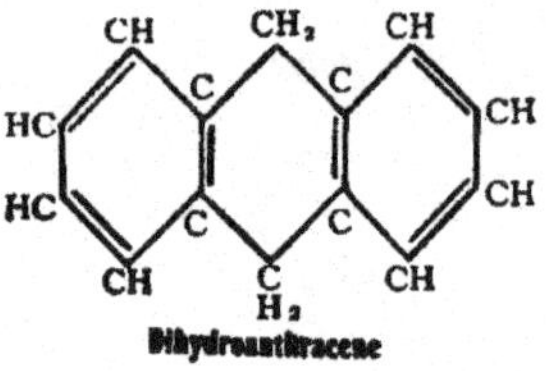

Dihydroanthracene

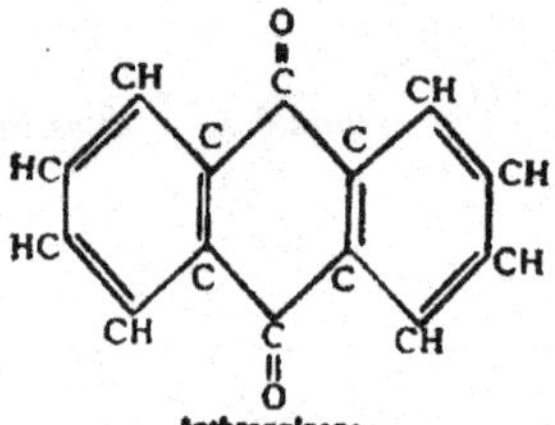

Anthraquinone

[1] Ann., 408, p. 122.

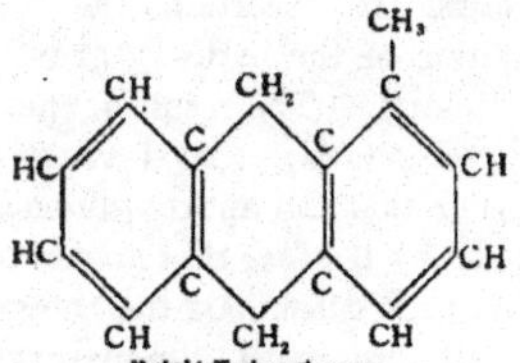

Methyl-1-dihydroanthracene

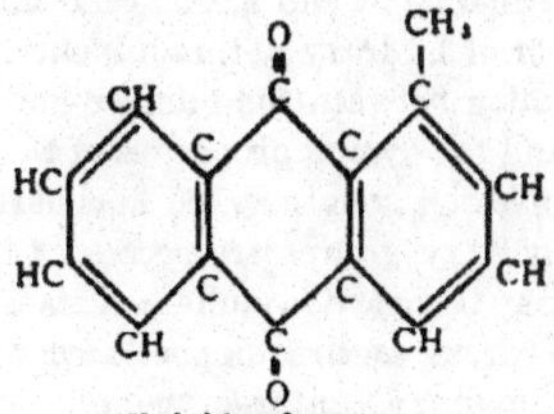

Methyl-1-anthraquinone

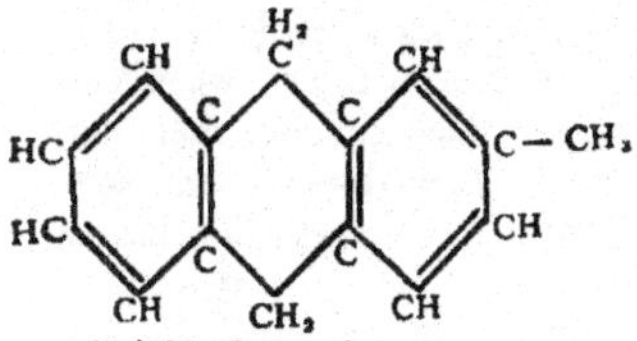

Methyl-2-dihydroanthracene

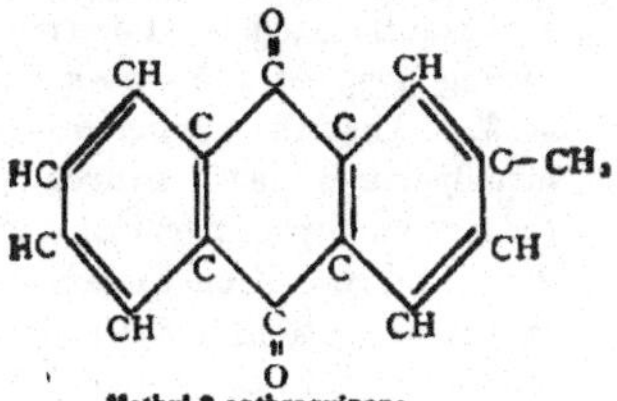

Methyl-2-anthraquinone

There exist in plants a large number of compounds, referable to these three hydrocarbons, most of which are used as dyestuffs. So far as is known, all except possibly the aloins, are hydroxy derivatives, and their alkyl or sugar ethers, of quinone oxidation products of these hydrocarbons, viz. anthraquinone and methyl anthraquinones. The aloins are possibly hydroxy derivatives of dihydro methyl anthracene.

Anthraquinone, which forms pale yellow crystals, is a quinone having its two carbonyl groups in p - position with reference to each other, a configuration which in itself is supposed to give color to a molecule. The intensity of the color, and especially the dyeing property, of the substance appears to depend upon the number and the position of free hydroxy groups introduced into the molecule.

As in the xanthone and flavone groups the compound appears to be more highly colored and to possess better dyeing properties when there is a hydroxy group in position -1- relatively ortho to the carbonyl group, so the anthraquinone pigments used particularly as dyes contain at least one hydroxy group in ortho position to one of the quinone oxygens. In 1887

Liebermann and Kostanecki[1] undertook a study of a large number of hydroxy anthraquinones in order to ascertain the relation between the number and position of the hydroxy groups and the dyeing properties of the compound. The result of their investigations may be summarized as follows: At least two hydroxy groups are necessary in order that the anthraquinones may become dye stuffs. This is shown by the fact that no monohydroxy anthraquinones have dyeing properties. Of the known dihydroxy anthraquinones, only alizarin with the hydroxy groups in positions 1 and 2 has strong dyeing properties. Hystazarin, which was not known at this time, 2, 3, dihydroxy anthraquinone, does, it is true, combine with mordants but its dyeing properties are weak and it is not satisfactory as a dye stuff. That the dyeing property of alizarin is not dependent on only one of the two hydroxy groups is shown by the fact that the monomethyl or mono ethyl ether of alizarin does not dye mordanted fabrics. From these facts Liebermann draws the conclusion that in order to have dyeing properties the polyhydroxy anthraquinones must have two of their hydroxy groups in positions 1 and 2.

All of the known trihydroxy anthraquinones which have the property of dyeing mordanted fabrics have two of their hydroxy groups in positions 1 and 2 or in similar positions. The same holds true for the tetrahydroxy derivatives. Those with hydroxy groups in positions 1, 4, 1′, 4′, have no dyeing properties whatever, and those with hydroxy groups in 1, 3, 2′, 4′, possess very weak dyeing properties. It is theoretically impossible to have pent- and hexhydroxy derivatives in which two of the hydroxy groups are not connected to carbon atoms in position 1 and 2. All of the known pent- and hexhydroxy anthraquinones are good dye stuffs.

An exception to Liebermann's rule seems to be found in chrysophanic acid. The formula for chrysophanic most favored at present represents the compound as possessing two hydroxy groups in positions 1′ - 4′, while none of the formulas considered have hydroxy groups in positions 1 - 2.

Although Liebermann has shown that all the hydroxyanthraquinones which have dyeing properties, with possibly a few exceptions, have hydroxy groups in positions 1 and 2, he has

[1] Ann., 240, p. 245.

apparently made no attempt to explain why this is so. Brandel[1] in his monograph on Plant Pigments offers such an explanation.

"It is well known that the mordants which are used in dyeing with these substances are salts of aluminum, iron and chromium, in other words salts of trivalent metals. The process of dyeing with mordants depends upon the formation of the aluminum, iron or chromium derivative and its deposition in the fiber. This being true, one would possibly not expect the monohydroxyanthraquinones to have dyeing properties, inasmuch as the union of three molecules of the monohydroxyanthraquinone with one atom of aluminum, might hardly be expected to take place very readily.

"On the other hand, by the introduction of more OH groups into the same molecule the tendency to form these trivalent metallic derivatives would be increased and it would be expected to be the greatest in those cases in which the OH groups are connected to neighboring carbon atoms. The bonds of the aluminum atom would be subject to a less strain as it were, than when they united with bonds from different molecules or from widely separated bonds in the same molecule. From this standpoint, the 2, 3, dihydroxyanthraquinone

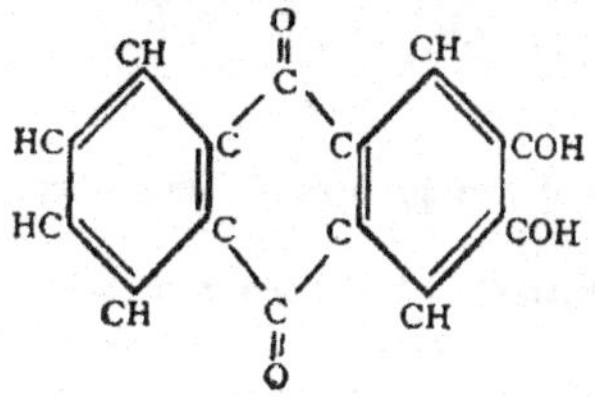

as well as the 1, 2, dihydroxyanthraquinone

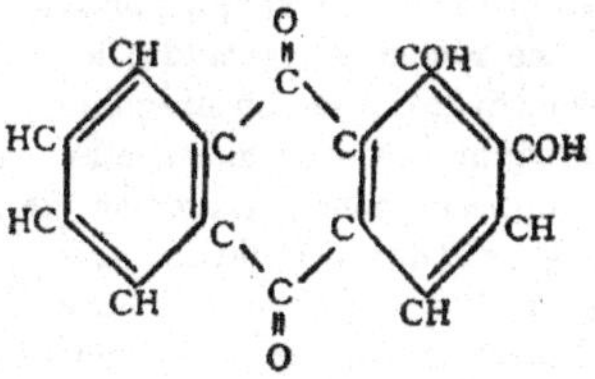

[1] Brandel—Plant Pigments, p. 29.

should have dyeing. properties. Both of these compounds are dyestuffs, the former not agreeing with the rule as laid down by Liebermann.

"In those compounds in which the OH groups are not connected to neighboring carbons atoms as is the case in the dihydroxanthraquinones, 1, 3, 1, 4; 1, 5, etc., the separation of the OH groups from one another decreases the tendency to form metallic derivatives with trivalent metals and therefore these compounds have no dyeing properties.

"On the basis of the same reasoning, the least strain of all would result and, therefore, an aluminum, iron or chromium derivative would be most readily formed in those cases in which there are three OH groups connected to neighboring carbon atoms. This is substantiated by the fact that anthragallol, 1, 2, 3, trihydroxanthraquinone.

has more intense dyeing properties than alizarin, 1, 2, dihydroxy derivative."

Of greater interest to the biochemist, however, than the relation of number and position of hydroxy groups to the color and dyeing properties of the compound is the coexistence of a number of these closely related compounds in the same or closely related plants and the possibility of the formation of one from another, or of all of them from simpler products of plant metabolism. From the root of *Oldenlandia umbellata* there have been isolated monohydroxy -2- anthraquinone; alizarin, dihydroxy -1, 2--anthraquinone and its monomethyl ether; hystazarin, dihydroxy -2, 3- anthraquinone and its monomethyl ether; anthragallol, -1, 2, 3- trihydroxy anthraquinone and three of its dimethyl ethers (A. B. C.). From *Rubia tinctorium* there have been isolated alizarin, dihydroxy -1, 2- anthraquinone; xanthopurpurin dihydroxy -1, 3- anthraquinone; purpurin, trihydroxy

1-, 2, 4-anthraquinone; rubiadin, methyl -1-dihydroxy -2, 4-anthraquinone; and pseudo purpurin, trihydroxy -1, 2, 4-methyl -2- anthraquinone, all as glucosides. In several other instances several of these anthraquinone derivatives are known to exist side by side in the plant. In *Rheum officinale* are found emodin, isoemedin, rhein and chrysophanic acid, while in *Rhamnus purshiana* are found emodine, chrysophanic acid and chrysarobin, a reduction product of chrysophanic acid. Of how the plants build up any or all of these related compounds, or pass from one to the other, nothing appears to be known. By the aid of structural formulae it can be shown how the plant might be able to synthesize anthraquinone from two molecules of carbonic acid and two of benzene.

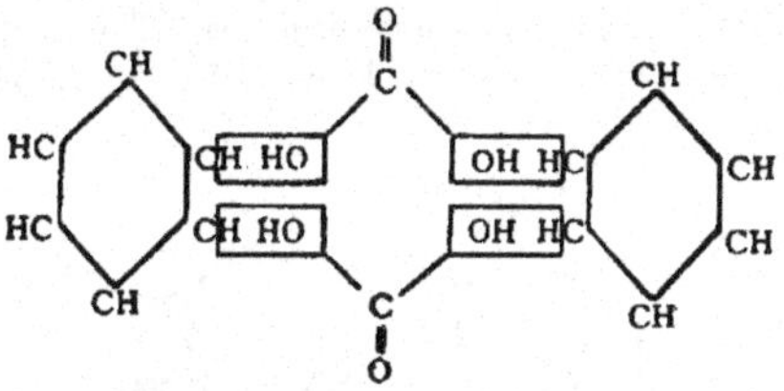

```
                            O
                            ‖
         CH                 C                 CH
   HC         CH HO               OH HC              CH
   HC         CH HO               OH HC              CH
         CH                 C                 CH
                            ‖
                            O
```

By the substitution of phenols or homologues of benzene for one or both of the benzene molecules the various anthraquinone pigments might be formed. Unfortunately for the probability of any such hypothesis little or nothing is known of the volatile constitutents of the anthraquinone producing plants. A large number of them contain tannic acid, gallic acid, and cinnamic acid however. By the condensation of two molecules of gallic acid a molecule of the anthraquinone configuration with six hydroxy groups would result.

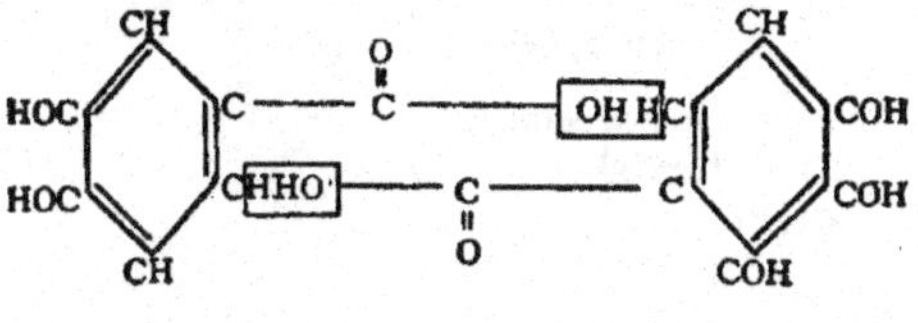

```
       CH                                      CH
                        O
                        ‖
 HOC          C ——— C ————— OH HC                  COH
 HOC          CHHO ——— C ————— C                   COH
                        ‖
                        O
       CH                                      COH
```

Unfortunately, again, such an anthraquinone derivative has not been isolated from plants. By the substitution of a molecule of benzoic acid for one of gallic acid anthragallol results, and by substituting benzoic acid or its homologues, and various hydroxy benzoic acids for the gallic acid molecules any of the anthraquinone derivatives might be produced, just as any of the xanthone derivatives might be obtained by condensation of a molecule of benzoic acid or its derivatives with a phenol or of two molecules of phenols with one of carbonic acid.

II. A. *Pigments referable to dihydroanthracene.*

Six plant pigments of known constitution are referable to dihydroanthracene as the underlying hydrocarbon. These are all anthraquinone pigments, being mono- di- and tri- hydroxy derivatives of anthraquinone. The relation of anthraquinone to dihydroanthracene is shown on page 108. The position of the hydroxy groups is here indicated by numbers in the usual way.

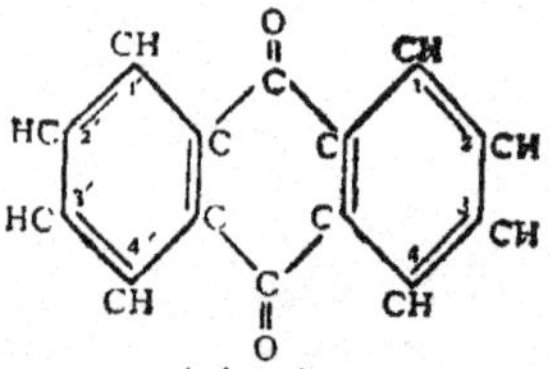

Anthraquinone

1.) Monohydroxyanthraquinones
    Monohydroxy -2- anthraquinone

2.) Dihydroxyanthraquinones
    a.) Alizarin
    b.) Hystazarin
    c.) Xanthopurpurin

3.) Trihydroxyanthraquinones
    a.) Anthragallol
    b.) Purpurin

II. A. 1.) *Monohydroxy anthraquinone pigments.*

Of this group of dihydroanthracene derivatives only one representative, the monohydroxy -2- anthraquinone, is known.

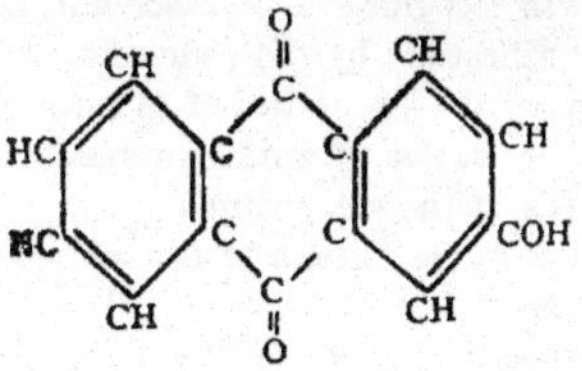

O
CH C CH
HC C C CH
HC C C COH
CH C CH
O

Monohydroxy -2- anthraquinone was first isolated from *Oldenlandia umbellata* by Perkin and Hummel[1] in 1893. It crystallizes in glistening yellow needles which melt at 302°. Solutions of the alkali hydrates dissolve it, forming a red liquid from which it separates, when very concentrated, in thin red plates of the corresponding salts. Sulphuric acid dissolves it with a red color.

Monohydroxy -2- anthraquinone does not combine with mordants to form a dye.

II. A. 2.) *Dihydroxy anthraquinone pigments.*

Of this group of dihydroanthracene derivatives three representatives have been isolated from plants. These are dihydroxy -1, 2- anthraquinone, alizarin; dihydroxy -2, 3- anthraquinone, hystazarin; and dihydroxy -1, 3- anthraquinone, xanthopurpurin.

Alizarin—Dihydroxy -1, 2- anthraquinone.

O
CH C COH
HC C C COH
HC C C CH
CH C CH
O

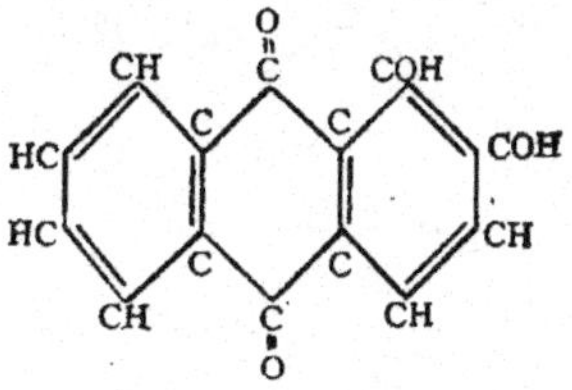

[1] Jr. Chem. Soc., 63, p. 1178; 67. 820.

Alizarin, the first known pigment of this group was discovered by Colin and Robiquet[1] in 1826 in the rhizom of *Rubia tinctorium* where it exists principally as the glucoside ruberythric acid. This glucoside was isolated by Rochleder[2] and Schunk[3] almost simultaneously in 1851. The relationship of alizirin to anthracene was recognized by Graebe and Liebermann[4] when they obtained anthracene by the reduction of alizarin. After a further study of the properties of alizarin they were able to pronounce it a derivative of anthraquinone. In 1869 they effected a synthesis of the compound.

Alizarin occurs in the rhizom of *Oldenlandia umbellata,*[5] and *Rubia tinctorium.*[1]

Alizarin crystallizes in red needles which melt at 289°–290°. It sublimes in orange red needles. It is easily soluble in alcohol and carbon disulphide but difficultly soluble in water. It dissolves in alkaline solutions with a violet blue color. Sulphuric acid dissolves it unchanged: Alizarin combines with most mordants. To cotton mordanted with aluminum it gives a garnet red color; with tin, a light red; with iron, violet; with chromium, a brownish purple color.

o–*Methyl alizarin*—The methyl ether of alizarin occurs with alizarin in the root of *Oldenlandia-umbellata,*[6] and in *Morinda longiflora.*[7] It crystallizes in orange colored crystals which melt at 178°. It does not dye mordanted fabrics, but it dissolves in solutions of the alkalies, also barium and calcium hydroxide with a red color.

Hystazarin, 2, 3- Dihydroxyanthraquinone.

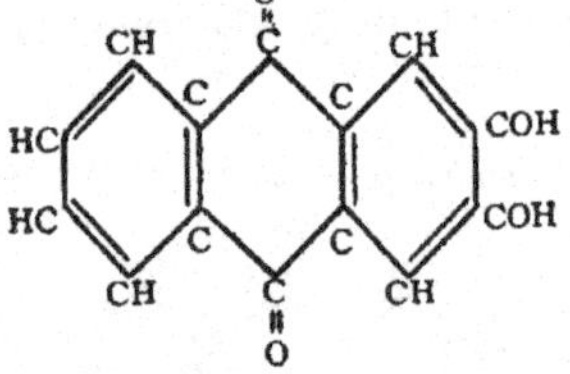

O
CH C CH
C C
HC COH
HC COH
C C
CH C CH
O

[1] Ann. chim. phys., (2) 34, p. 225.
[2] Ann., 80, p. 321.
[3] Ann., 81, p. 336.
[4] Ber., 2, p. 332.
[5] Proc. Chem. Soc., 23, p. 288.
[6] Jr. Chem. Soc.. 64, p. 1160.
[7] Jr. Chem. Soc.. 91, p. 1913; Proc. Chem. Soc., 23, p. 248.

Hystazarin exists in the Chay root, *Oldenlandia umbellata*,[1] in the form of its monomethyl ether.

Hystazarin crystallizes in orange yellow needles which melt at 260°. It is difficultly soluble in hot alcohol, ether, acetone, and acetic acid; insoluble in benzene and toluene; soluble in solutions of alkalies with a blue color, of ammonia with violet, and of acids with a red color. It forms a dark violet calcium[2] salt and a dark blue barium salt. It is not satisfactory as a dye.[3]

Hystazarin monomethyl ether crystallizes in orange yellow needles which melt at 232°. It is soluble in alkalies with a red color.

Xanthopurpurin or Purpuroxanthin.

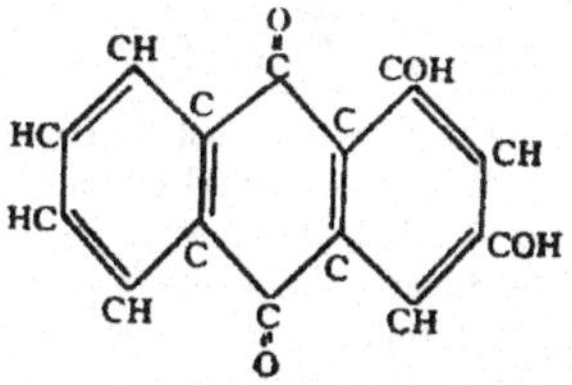

Xanthopurpurin the dihydroxy -1, 3- anthraquinone exists in the rhizome of *Rubia tinctorium*.[1]

Xanthopurpurin crystallizes in yellow needles and sublimes in yellowish red needles. It melts at 262°–263°. It is easily soluble in alcohol, benzene, and acetic acid. By heating with alkali in contact with air it is transformed into purpurin, trihydroxy -1, 2, 4- anthraquinone. Xanthopurpurin imparts a rather fugitive yellow color to fabrics mordanted with aluminum.

---

[1] Proc. Chem. Soc., 23, p. 228; Jr. Chem. Soc., 63, p. 1160.
[2] Ber., 28, p. 118.
[3] Ber., 35, p. 1778; 21, p. 2501.
[1] Bull. Soc., Chim., 4, p. 12.
[2] Ann. de Chim. et de Phys., (5) 18, p. 224.

II. A. 3.) *Trihydroxyanthraquinone pigments.*

Of this group of dihydroanthracene derivatives two representatives are known in plants, trihydroxy -1, 2, 3- anthraquinone or anthragallol, and trihydroxy -1, 2, 4- anthraquinone or purpurin.

Anthragallol—Trihydroxy—1, 2, 3—anthraquinone.

O
C
CH CH
C C
HC COH
HC COH
C C
CH C C
O COH

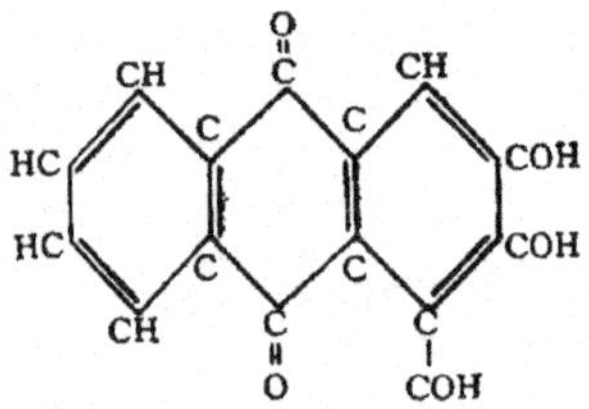

Anthragallol exists in the Chay root, ***Oldenlandia umbellata,***[1] in the form of three different dimethyl ethers, the dimethyl-1, 3-ether, known as the A ether, the dimethyl-1, 2-ether, known as the B ether, and the dimethyl-2, 3-ether, known as the C ether.[2]

Anthragallol itself forms orange red crystals and is an excellent dye stuff, producing the anthracene brown of commerce. Its monomethyl-3-ether no longer colors mordanted fabrics brown, but in shades of red similar to those produced by alizarin. The two dimethyl ethers have no dyeing properties.

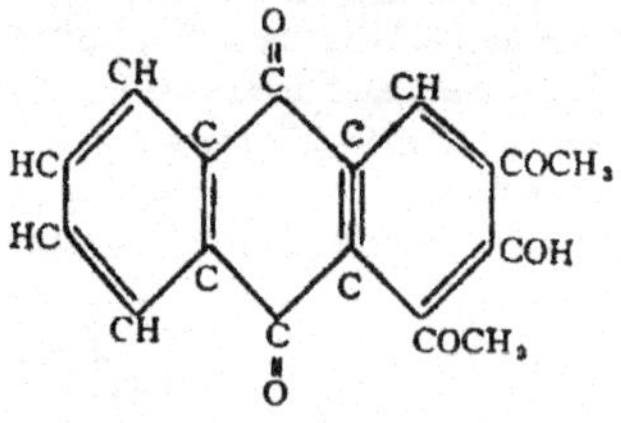

O
C
CH CH
C C
HC $COCH_3$
HC COH
C C
CH C $COCH_3$
O

Anthragallol dimethyl ether A, Dimethoxy-1,-3-hydroxy-2-anthraquinone.

[1] Jr. Chem. Soc., 63, p. 1160; 91, p. 2066.
[2] Jr. Chem. Soc., 67, p. 826.

This compound is found in the root of *Oldenlandia umbellata.*[1] It crystallizes in yellow needles which melt at 209°. It is slightly soluble in alcohol and acetic acid, insoluble in chloroform and carbon disulphide. In solutions of alkaline carbonates it dissolves with a bright red color. It has no dyeing properties.

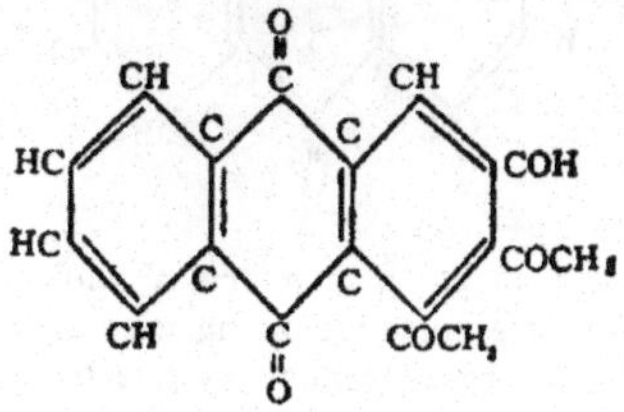

O
CH C CH
C C
HC COH
HC $COCH_3$
C C
CH C $COCH_3$
O

Anthragallol dimethyl ether B, Dimethoxy-1, 2-hydroxy-3-anthraquinone.

This compound occurs also in the root of *Oldenlandia umbellata.* It crystallizes in long pale straw colored crystals which melt at 230°–232° and are difficultly soluble in alcohol, acetic acid, and ether; but soluble in alkali solutions with a red color.

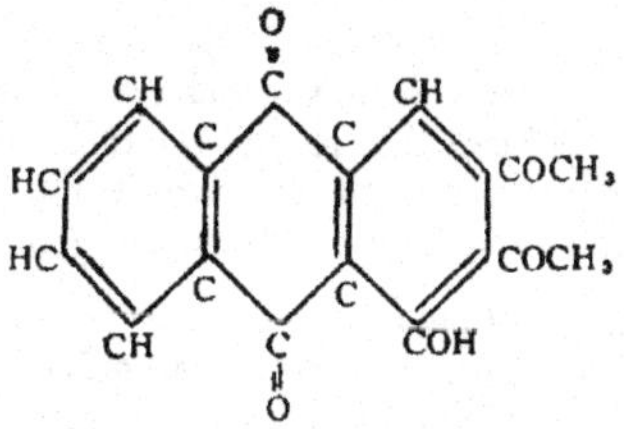

O
CH C CH
C C
HC $COCH_3$
HC $COCH_3$
C C
CH C COH
O

Anthragallol dimethyl ether C, Dimethoxy-2, 3-hydroxy-1-anthraquinone.

This third dimethyl ether also occurs in the root of *Oldenlandia umbellata.* It forms a barium salt melting at 212°–213° and a lead salt.

Purpurin,—Trihydroxy-1, 2, 4-anthraquinone.

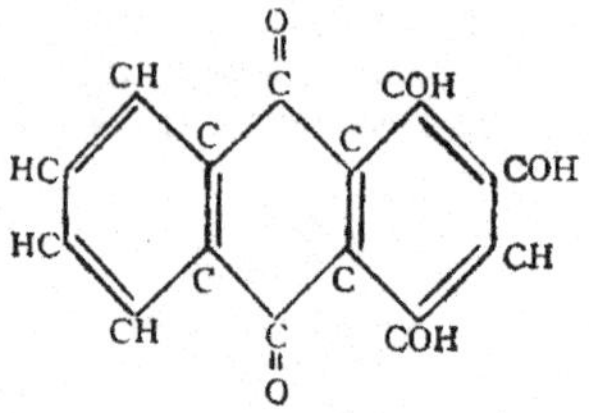

O
CH C COH
C C
HC COH
HC CH
C C
CH C COH
O

Purpurin exists in *Rubia tinctorium*[1] and other species of *Rubia*,[2] probably as a glucoside, along with alizarin. Purpurin crystallizes in long orange yellow crystals which melt at 253°. It is soluble in water with a deep yellow color, soluble in ether and carbon disulphide, acetic acid and hot benzene; but almost insoluble in alkaline solutions. It imparts to fabrics mordanted with aluminum a violet red color, with iron a violet blue, and with chromium a reddish brown color. These colors are not so permanent as those given by alizarin.

II. B.) *Pigments referable to the homologues of dihydroanthracene.*

The plant pigments referable to the homologues of dihydroanthracene are derivatives of two different monomethyl ethers of dihydroanthracene, the methyl-1-anthraquinone and the methyl-2-anthraquinone. Of the former five representatives and of the latter three representatives are found in plants.

1. Methyl-1-anthraquinone.
   - a.) Dihydroxy methyl-1-anthraquinones.
     - Rubiadin.
     - Chrysophanic acid.
   - b.) Trihydroxy methyl-1-anthraquinones.
     - Emodin.
     - Aloeemodin.
   - c.) Penthydroxy methyl-1-anthraquinones.
     - Rhein.

---

[1] Ann., 2, p. 34; Jr. prakt. Chem., 5, p. 366; Ann., 66, p. 351.
[2] Jr. Chem. Soc., 63, p. 1157.

2. Methyl-2-anthraquinone.
   a.) Trihydroxy methyl-2-anthraquinones.
   Morindon.
   b.) Hexhydroxy methyl-2-anthraquinones.
   Pseudo purpurin.

II. B. 1.) *Pigments referable to methyl-1-dihydroanthracene.*

Five pigments of known constitution are referable to methyl-1-anthraquinone. These are rubiadin, a dihydroxy-2, 4-methyl-1-anthraquinone; chrysophanic acid, a dihydroxy-1′, 4′-methyl-1-anthraquinone; emodin, a trihydroxy-3, 1′, 4′-methyl-1-anthraquinone; aloeemodin, a trihydroxy-3, 4′, 5-methyl-1-anthraquinone, and rhein, a dihydroxy-3, 4′-carboxy-1-anthraquinone.

Dihydroxides of methyl-1-anthraquinone.

Two pigments which are dihydroxides of methyl-1-anthraquinone are known to exist in plants. These are rubiadin, dihydroxy-2, 4-methyl-1-anthraquinone, and chrysophanic acid, dihydroxy-1′, 4′-methyl-1-anthraquinone. As would be expected from their similar constitutions the two compounds resemble each other quite closely in properties, though chrysophanic acid has the better dyeing properties. The fact that chrysophanic acid possesses dyeing properties appears to be an exception to Liebermann's rule regarding the relation between dyeing properties and the number and position of hydroxy groups, since of the three structural formulae assigned to it by different investigators none have the two hydroxy groups in relatively 1, 2, positions, while the formula which appears to be preferred at present has its hydroxy group in 1′, 4′, relatively para position, a position which is supposed to give no dyeing properties to anthraquinone derivatives.

Rubiadin,—Dihydroxy-2, 4-methyl-1-anthraquinone.

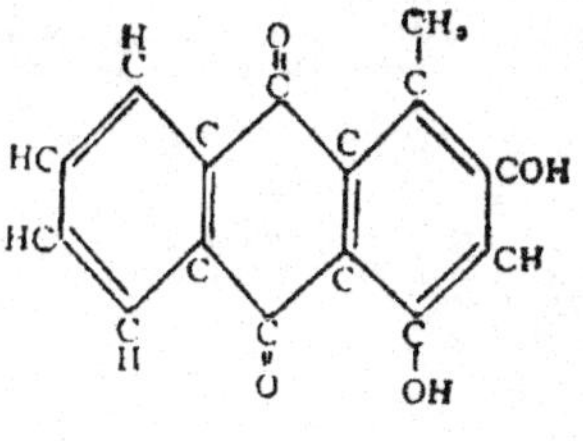

Rubiadin occurs as a glucoside in the root of ***Rubia tinctorium.***[1] It crystallizes in yellow needles which melt at 290°. It is easily soluble in alcohol, ether, and benzene, but insoluble in water and carbon disulphide, also in lime water. In solutions of alkalies it dissolves with a red color.

Chrysophanic acid,—Dihydroxy-1', 4'-methyl-1-anthraquinone (?).

I.

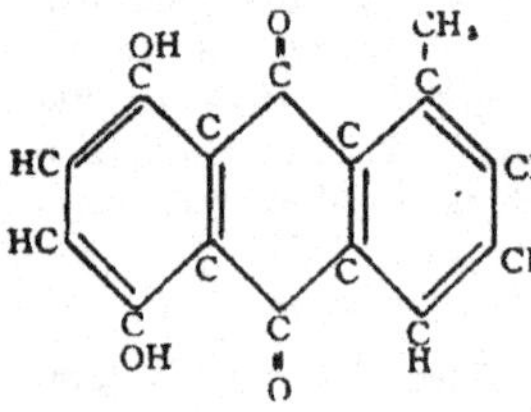

II.

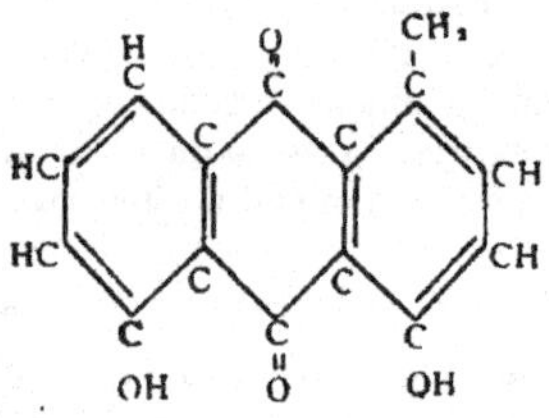

III.

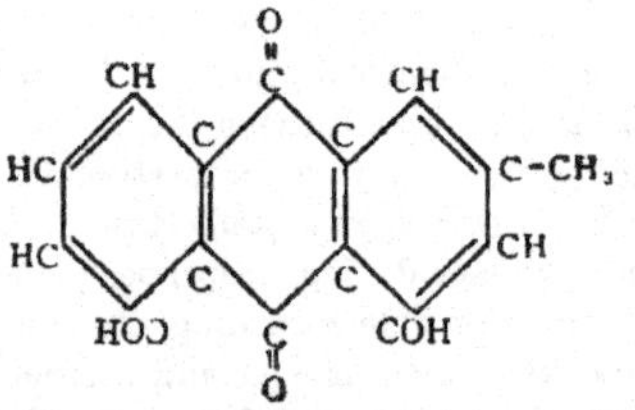

Chrysophanic acid occurs in the root of ***Rheum officinale,***[1] ***Rheum rhaponticum,***[2] ***Rumex obtusifolius,***[3] ***Rumex ecklonianus,***[3] ***Cassia angustifolia,***[5] ***Cassia speciosa,***[4] ***Rhamnus purshiana,***[7] ***Rhamnus japonica,***[6] ***Rhamnus frangula,***[6] and ***Tecoma ochraceae.***[8]

Chrysophanic acid crystallizes in yellow leaflets and melts at 196°. It is insoluble in water, soluble in alcohol, ether, acetone, benzene, chloroform, and petroleum ether. These so-

---

[1] Jr. Chem. Soc., 63, p. 969, 1137; 65, p. 182; Chem. News, 67, p. 299.

[1] Ann., 309, p. 32; Arch. d. Pharm., 245, p. 680; Ann., 9, p. 85; 50, p. 196; 107, p. 324.

[2] Berl. Jahres., 23, p. 252; Jahresb. f. Pharm., 1882, p. 262.

[3] Jr. Chem. Soc., 97, p. 1.

[4] Arch. Pharm., 184, p. 37.

[5] Chem. Centralbl., 1864, p. 622; Jr. Pharm. Chim., 12, p. 505.

[6] Apoth. Ztg., 15, p. 587; 16, p. 257, 538; 17, p. 372.

[7] Proc. A. Ph. A., 52, p. 288.

[8] Z. oester. Apoth. Ver., 12, p. 31.

lutions color animal tissues deep yellow. It is soluble in solutions of alkaline hydroxides with a red color. Chrysophanic acid colors unmordanted silk and wool yellow. Wools mordanted with aluminum are colored orange red; with chromium, bright red; and with iron, bright brown.

The constitution[*] of chrysophanic acid is probably as indicated in formula I. above. This formula was first suggested by Hesse in 1899, and afterwards by Jowett and Potter in 1903. Attention should here be called to the fact that none of the above formulae are in accord with Liebermann's rule for a colored molecule.

The principal investigations of chrysophanic acid are mentioned in the following list:

Literature on Chrysophanic Acid.

Aweng, — Pharm. Centralbl., 1898, p. 776; Apoth. Ztg., 15, p. 537; 17, p. 372.
Brandes, — Ann., 9, p. 85.
Dulk, — Arch. d. Pharm., 17, II. p. 26.
Geiger, — Ann., 9, p. 91.
Gilson, — Arch. internat. de Pharm et Therap., 11, p. 487.
Grandis, — Jahresb. d. Chem., 1892 p. 1654.
Grothe, — Chem. Centralbl., 1862, p. 107.
Hesse, — Ann., 291, p. 306; 309, p. 32.
Jowett and Potter, — Jr. Chem. Soc., 81, p. 1528; 83, p. 1327.
Le Prince, — C. r., 129, p. 60.
Liebermann, — Ann., 183, p. 169; 212, p. 36; Ber., 11, p. 1607.
Limousin, — Jr. de Pharm et de Chem., 1885, p. 80.
Marfori, — Chem. Centrlbl., 1900, I. p. 1292.
Oesterle, — Arch. d. Pharm., 243, p. 434.
Pelz, — Jahresber. d. Chem., 1861, p. 392.
Rochleder, — Ber., 2, p. 373.
Rue and Mueller, — Jahresber d. Chem., 1857, p. 516.
Rupe, — Chem. der nat. Farbs., 2, p. 117.
Schoeller, — Ber., 32, p. 683.
Scholzberger, — Ann., 50, p. 196.
Thann. — Ann., 107, p. 324.
Tschirch and Cristofoletti, — Arch. d. Pharm., 243, p. 434.

[*] Jr. Chem. Soc., 83, p. 1327; Ann., 309, p. 32.

Tschirch and Heuberger, — Arch. d. Pharm., 240, p. 605.
Tschirch, — B., 8, p. 189.
Tutin and Clewer, — Jr. Chem. Soc., 97, p. 1.
Vogel, — Arch. d. Pharm., 134, p. 37 (1868).

Trihydroxides of methyl-1-anthraquinone.

Two trihydroxides of methyl-1-anthraquinone, emodin, and aloeemodin, are known to exist in plants. These two isomeric pigments occur together in various species of aloes and senna, along with chrysophanic acid, of which emodin is a hydroxy substitution product.

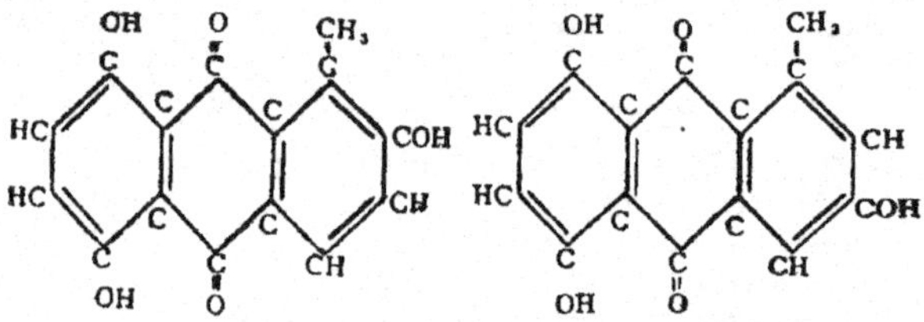

Emodin,[1] a methyl -1-trihydroxy-2, 1′, 4′-anthraquinone, or methyl-1-trihydroxy-3, 1′, 4′-anthraquinone is an hydroxy substitution product of chrysophanic acid.

Emodin occurs in various species of aloe,[2] including *Aloe ferox,*[3] *Aloe vulgaris,*[4] and *Aloe chinensis;*[5] in *Rheum officinale,*[6] *Rheum palmatum,*[7] *Polygonum cuspidatum,*[8] *Cassia occidentalis,*[9] *Cassia sophora,*[9] *Cassia tora,*[10] *Cassia angustifolia,*[9] *Xanthoxylon tingoassuiba,*[11] *Rhamnus cathartica,*[12] *Rhamnus japonica,*[13] *Rhamnus purshiana,*[14] and *Rhamnus frangula,*[15]

---

[1] Jr. Chem. Soc., 83, p. 1327.
[2] Jr. Pharm. Chim., 28, p. 529.
[3] B. Pharm. Ges., 1898, p. 174.
[4] Arch. Pharm., 236, p. 200.
[5] Arch. Pharm., 241, p. 340.
[6] C. r., 136, p. 385.
[7] Ber., 1882, p. 902; Pharm. Jr. Trans., 15, p. 136.
[8] Bull. Sci. Pharm., 14, p. 698.
[9] Apoth. Ztg., 1896, p. 537.
[10] Pharm. Jr. Trans., 8, p. 242.
[11] B. Pharm. Ges., 9., p. 162.
[12] Jr. Russ. Phys. Chem. Ges., 40, p. 1502.
[13] Apoth. Ztg., 1896, p. 537.
[14] Arch. Pharm., 246, p. 315; Jr. Pharm. Chem., 246, p. 315.
[15] Ber., 9, p. 1775; Pharm. Jr., 20, p. 558; Arch. Pharm., 246, p. 315.

It will be seen from the above that emodin not only resembles chrysophanic acid in constitution but closely accompanies it in the plant as well. Emodin occurs both free and as a glucoside. It crystallizes in silky needles of an orange red color which melts at 250°. It is soluble in alcohol, amyl alcohol, and acetic acid, slightly soluble in benzene, and soluble in alkalies and ammonia with a red color. With sulphuric acid it gives an intense red solution which turns yellow, separates a flocculent precipitate, and becomes colorless upon standing.

A considerable number of derivatives of emodin have been prepared.

The principal investigators of emodin are listed below.

Combes, — Bull. de Soc. Chem., (4) 1, p. 800.
Hesse, — Ann., 284, p. 194; 309, p. 41.
Krassowski, — Jr. d. russ. phys. chem., Ges., 40, p. 510; Chem. Centrlbl. 1919, I. p. 773.
Le Prince, — C. r., 129, p. 60.
Liebermann, — B., 9, p. 1775; 21, p. 436.
Oesterle, — Arch. d. Pharm., 237, p. 699.
Oesterle and Tisza, — Arch. d. Pharm., 246, p. 112, 432; Chem. Centrlbl. 1908, I. p. 1548; II. p. 1441.
Tschirch and Pool, — Arch. d. Pharm., 246, p. 315.
Warren — Jr., Chem. Soc., 10, p. 100.
Rochleder, — B., 2, p. 373.

Frangulin.[1]—A glucoside of emodin, known as frangulin, occurs in the bark of *Rhamnus frangula.*[2] It crystallizes in lemon yellow crystals which melt at 226°. It is insoluble in water and in ether, soluble in alcohol and in benzene. Upon hydrolysis it yields emodin and rhamnose.[3]

Polygonin.—A second glucoside of emodin, known as polygonin, occurs in the root of *Polygonum cuspidatum.*[4] It crystallizes in fine orange yellow needles which melt at 202°–203°. It is insoluble in water, difficultly soluble in alcohol, also in hot water. When hydrolized it yields emodin and a sugar.

---

[1] C. r., 134.
[2] Rep. f. Pharm., 104, p. 151; Ann., 104, p. 77.
[3] Ann., 165, p. 230.
[4] Jr. Chem. Soc., 67, p. 1084.

Aloeemodin.—Trihydroxy-2, 4′, 5-hydroxymethyl-1-anthraquinone.

O CH₂OH
CH C C
C C
HC COH
HC CH
C C
C C CH
OH O

Aloeemodin, a primary alcohol, occurs with aloin in various species of aloes,[1] senna[2] and rhubarb.[3] It crystallizes in orange red needles which melt at 224°. It is easily soluble in ether, hot alcohol, and benzene, soluble in concentrated sulphuric acid with a cherry red color. Aloeemodin yields a triacetyl and a tribenzoyl derivative. Upon reduction it forms methyl anthracene. Oxidized with chromic acid mixture it yields rhein.

O COOH
CH C C
C C
HC CH
HC COH
C C
C C CH
OH O

Since rhein is produced upon the oxidation of aloeemodin, one of its hydroxy groups must be in the side chain. The positions of the other hydroxy groups is uncertain. Robinson and Simonson[4] have suggested for it the formula given above.

Penthydroxides of methyl-1-anthraquinone.

Only one penthydroxide of methyl-1-anthraquinone is known to exist in plants. This is rhein, a dihydroxyanthraquinone carboxylic acid. Rhein is an oxidation product of aloeemodin which it accompanies in several species of aloes, and also of rhubarb.

---

[1] Whemer, Die Pflanzenstoffe, p. 90; C.r., 150, p. 983; Arch. f. Pharm., 247, p. 413.

[2] Rupe, Natuerliche Farbstoffe, 2, p. 134.

[3] Arch. Pharm., 248, p. 443; 247, p. 413.

[4] Proc. Chem. Soc., 25, p. 76; Jr. Chem. Soc., 95, p. 1085.

Rhein.—Dihydroxy-3, 4′-carboxyl-1-anthraquinone.

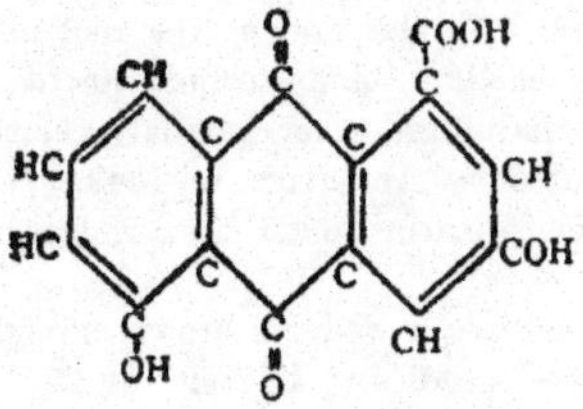

Rhein occurs in *Rheum officinale;*[1] English rhubarb;[2] *Rheum rhaponticum;*[3] *Rheum palmatum;*[4] and *Aloe vulgaris.*[5] It may be formed by oxidation of Aloeemodin which occurs with it in several species of Rhubarb.

Rhein crystallizes in small yellow needles which melt at 321°–322°. It is difficultly soluble in most ordinary solvents. It is soluble in concentrated sulphuric acid with a red color, also soluble in ammonia with a red color, upon exposure to the air this color goes through violet into blue. In dilute alkaline solutions it is readily soluble. Acids precipitate it from these solutions as a yellow mass. It forms esters[6] and ethers,[6] the former with alcohol, the latter with dimethyl sulphate in the presence of potassium hydroxide. It dyes wools mordanted with chromium a yellow color.[7]

The structural formula given is that suggested by Robinson and Simonsen.[6]

II. B. 2.) *Pigments referable to methyl-2-dihydroanthracene.*

a. Trihydroxides of methyl-2-anthraquinone.

One pigment which is a trihydroxide of methyl-2-anthraquinone is known to exist in plants, this is morindon.

b. Hexhydroxides of methyl-2-anthraquinone.

One pigment, pseudo purpurin, which is a hexhydroxide of methyl-2-anthraquinone, is known to exist in plants.

---

[1] Pharm. Post., 37, p. 233, Arch. Pharm., 245, p. 150.
[2] Arch. Pharm., 245, p. 141.
[3] Arch. Pharm., 243, p. 443.
[4] Schweiz. Wochenschs. Pharm., 1904. Nr. 40.
[5] Arch. Pharm., 247, p. 413.
[6] Jr. Chem. Soc., 95, p. 1085.
[7] Rupe. Natuerliche Farbstoffe, 2, p. 143.

Trihydroxides of methyl-2-anthraquinone.

Morindon,—A trihydroxy methyl-2-anthraquinone, isomeric with emodin, occurs in the rind of the root of ***Morinda citrifolia,***[1] ***Morinda umbellata,***[2] and ***Morinda tinctoria,***[3] along with the glucoside morindin and other similar coloring principles. It was first isolated by Anderson[1] in 1849. It has sometimes been mistaken for alizarin which it resembles in many of its properties.

Morindon crystallizes in reddish brown crystals and sublimes in long orange red needles. It melts at 272°. It is easily soluble in alcohol ether, ethyl acetate, benzene and similar hydrocarbons. Ferric chloride colors a solution of morindon dark green, alkalies a violet blue. Morindin is soluble in concentrated sulphuric acid with a violet blue color.

Literature on Morindin and Morindon.

Anderson, — Ann., 71, p. 216.
Oesterle and Tisza, — Arch. d. Pharm., 245, p. 534.
Perkin and Hummel, — Jr. Chem. Soc., 65, p. 851.
Rochleder, — Ann., 82, p. 205.
Stenhouse, — Jahresber. d. Chem., 97, p. 234.
Stockes, — Jahresber. d. Chem., 17, p. 543.
Stockes and Stein, — Jahresber. d. Chem., 19, p. 645.
Thorpe and Greenall, — Jahresber. d. Chem., 40, p. 2299.
Thorpe and Smith, — Jahresber. d. Chem., 40, p. 2363.
Tschirch, — Arch. d. Pharm., 222, p. 129.
Tunmann, — Chem. Centralbl., 1909. I. p. 199.

Hexhydroxides of methyl-2-anthraquinone.

Pseudopurpurin,—Trihydroxy-1, 2, 4-carboxyl-2′-anthraquinone, or Trihydroxy-1, 2, 4-carboxyl-3′-anthraquinone.

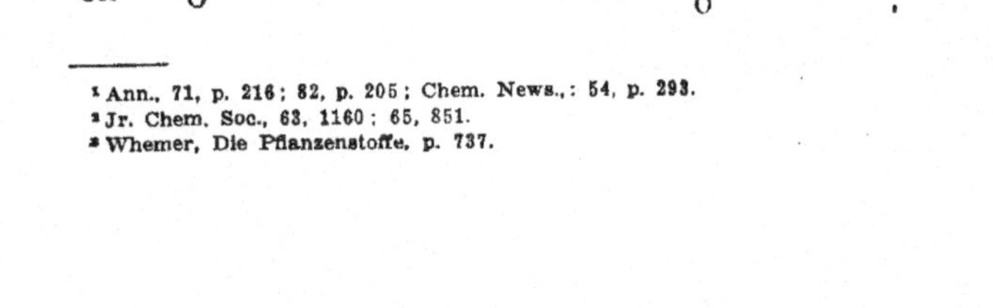

[1] Ann., 71, p. 216; 82, p. 205; Chem. News.,: 54, p. 293.
[2] Jr. Chem. Soc., 63, 1160; 65, 851.
[3] Whemer, Die Pflanzenstoffe, p. 737.

Pseudo purpurin occurs along with purpurin in the root of *Rubia tinctorium*,[1] It comprises a large part of the purpurin of commerce. The constitution of the molecule does not appear to have been yet definitely established. From the work of Rosenstiehl,[2] also that of Liebermann and Platt,[3] we learn the number and relative positions of the hydroxy groups. Perkin[4] has shown that the carboxyl group is in the second benzene nucleus, corresponding to one of the formulae given above.

Pseudo purpurin crystallizes in small red leaflets. It melts at 218°–219°. It is almost insoluble in water and in alcohol, difficultly soluble in chloroform and hot benzene, easily soluble in solutions of alkaline carbonates with an orange color. Its dyeing properties are almost identical with those of purpurin.

The Aloins.

Substances crystallizing in yellow needles and soluble in concentrated sulphuric acid with a red, in alkaline hydroxides and carbonates with an orange color, are found in various species of aloes. These are known as aloins. The formula of aloin has been variously given as $C_{16}H_{16}O_7$, $C_{16}H_{18}O_9$, $C_{17}H_{18}O_7$. According to Jowett and Potter who have performed some of the most recent work upon aloin, $C_{16}H_{18}O_7$ is probably correct.

The aloins, known as aloin, barbaloin, isobarbaloin, and nataloin are closely related to the anthraquinone pigments. Jowett and Potter think, however, that instead of the anthraquinone nucleus being present there is probably a reduced anthraquinone nucleus.

Upon treating aloin with sodium peroxide aloeemodin is produced.

III. PIGMENTS REFERABLE TO PHENYL-HYDRINDINE AND HOMOLOGUES.

CH, HC, HC, CH, C, C, C, H, C, C, γ, α, β, C–CH$_3$, C, H$_2$, CH CH, CH, CH CH

β-methyl- γ-phenyl hdyrindine

[1] Bull. Soc. Chim., 4, p. 12.
[2] C. r., 79, p. 680; 84, p. 559, 1902.
[3] Ber., 10, p. 1618.
[4] Jr. Chem. Soc, 65, p. 842.

No pigments referable to the above hydrocarbons are found in plants; but two pigment forming substances, brazilin and haematoxylin, which upon oxidation yield the pigments brazilein and haematein, are referable to it. The pigments themselves are referable to an isomer of methyl-phenyl hydrindine, falling under the same degree of saturation.

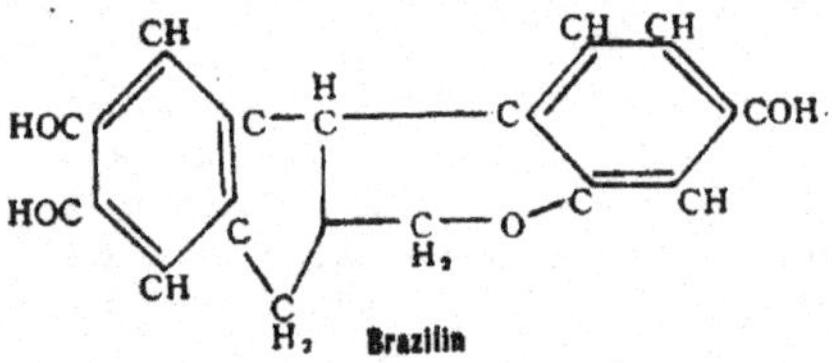

Brazilin

Brazilin was first discovered by Chevreul,[1] in 1808, in the heart wood of *Cisalpina echinata* where it exists in the form of a glucoside. It was not until one-hundred years later, however, that its constitution was definitely established when Perkin,[2] in 1908, after a long series of investigations, by the synthesis of brazilinic acid and other derivatives of brazilin, showed the formula to be that given above. Besides in *Cisalpina echinata*, brazilin occurs in another species of *Cisalpina*, *C. sappari.*[3] According to Rupe[4] a number of woods, known as red woods, employed as dyestuffs contain brazilin. These are all the products of varieties of *Cisalpinia* species and are known as Fernanabose or Brazil wood, Bahia red wood; St. Martha wood; Nicaragua wood, Sapan wood, Lima wood and Braziliette wood.

Brazilin crystallizes in colorless crystals which color readily upon exposure to the air. It is soluble in water, alcohol and ether, these solutions color quickly upon exposure to the air.

Brazilin and its derivatives have been the subject of a large number of chemical investigations, the principal ones of which are listed below.

---

[1] Ann. Chim. et Phys., 66, p. 225.
[2] Proc. Chem. Soc., 79, p. 1396; 81, p. 221, 235, 1008; 91, 1073; 93, p. 489.
[3] Ber., 5, p. 572.
[4] Chemie der natuerlichen Farbestoffe., 1, p. 224.

Literature on Brazilin.

Benedict, — Ann., 178, p. 100.
Bolley, — Schweiz polytech. Zeit., 9, p. 267.
Buchka, — Ber., 17, p. 685; 18, p. 1140.
Chevreul, — Ann. Chem. Phys., 66, p. 225.
Dralle,—Ber., 17, p. 375; 20, p. 3365; 21, p. 3009; 22, p. 1547; 23, p. 1430; 25, p. 3670; 27, p. 527.
Herzig, — Montsh. f. Chem., 19, p. 738; 23, p. 241; 25, p. 871.
Herzig and Pollak, — B. 36, p. 398.
Kostanecki, — Ber., 35, p. 1674; 36, p. 2202.
Liebermann and Burz, — B. 9, p. 1885.
Perkin, — Jr. Chem. Soc. 79, p. 1396; 81, p. 225, 1008, 1057; 91, p. 1073; 93, p. 489, 1115; 95, p. 385.
Rein, — Ber., 4, p. 334.
Schall, — B. 27, p. 529; 35, p. 2306.

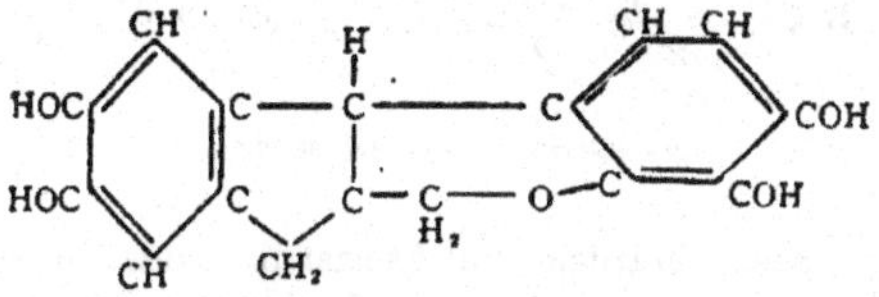

Haematoxlyn

Haematoxylin was discovered by Chevreul,[1] in 1812, in the heart of *Haematoxylon campechianum.* It has also been reported in the bark of *Sancta indica,*[2] another leguminous plant.

Haematoxylin, being a hydroxy brazilin, resembles it closely in physical and chemical properties. Its history also has been almost identical with that of brazilin since the work which proved the constitution of one compound proved also that of the other. According to Perkin[3] the formula of haematoxylin is as given above. Kostanecki and Lampe[4] have suggested another formula which differs only in the position of one benzene nucleus and one hydroxy group. The later formula of Perkin and his associates is probably to be preferred.

[1] Ann. Chim et Phys., 66, p. 225 (2) 82, p. 53, 126.
[2] Pharm. Post., 1887, p. 778.
[3] Jr. Chem. Soc., 93, p. 496.
[4] Ber., 35, p. 1674.

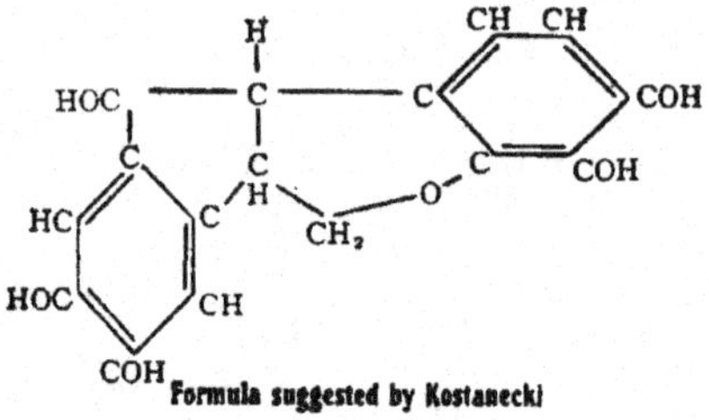

Formula suggested by Kostanecki

PIGMENTS REFERABLE TO β-METHYL-γ-PHENYL-ISOHYDRINDINE.

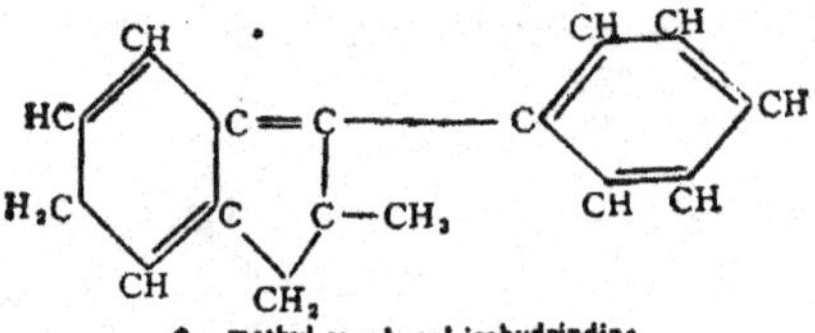

β- methyl-γ -phenyl isohydrindine

Two pigments, brazilein and haematein, oxidation products of brazilin and haematoxylin are referable to the above hydrocarbon.

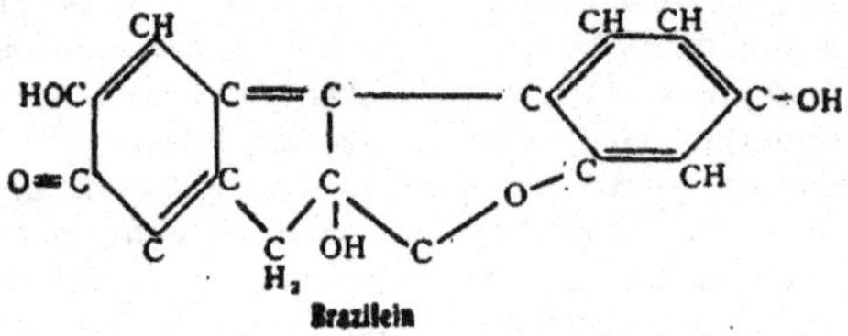

Brazilein

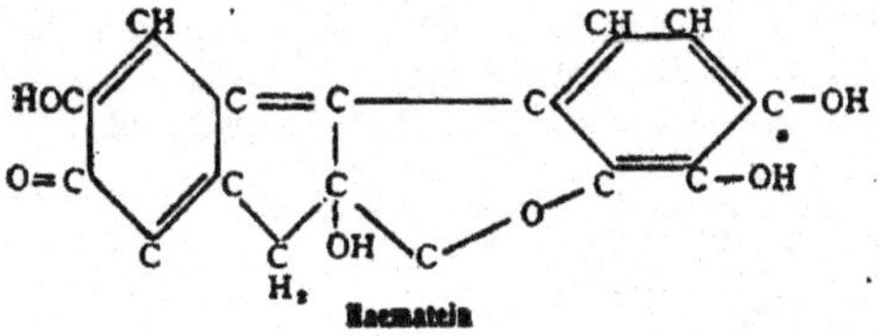

Haematein

Brazilein occurs along with brazilin in various species of "red wood," *Cisalpinia*. It crystallizes in microscopic reddish brown crystals with a metallic reflection. It is very slightly soluble in cold water, better in hot water. The solution is bright red with an orange fluorescence. It is soluble in alkaline solutions with a bright red color which turns brown upon standing in contact with the air.

Brazilein dyes fabrics mordanted with aluminum a blueish red; with chromium, grayish brown to violet gray; with tin, orange red; with iron and aluminum mixed, a dark purplish red.

Brazilein has been the subject of a large number of chemical investigations and a large number of derivatives have been prepared.

Literature on Brazilein.

Herzig, — Monatsh. f. Chem., 19, p. 739; 20, p. 461; 22, p. 207; 23, p. 165; 25, p. 734; 27, p. 743.

Kostanecki, — B., 32, p. 1042; 41, p. 2373.

Perkin, — Proc. Chem. Soc., 22, p. 132; 23, p. 291; 24, p. 54, 148; 93,, p. 489, 1115; 95, p. 381.

Liebermann, — Ber., 9, p. 1866.

Scholl and Dralle, — Ber., 17, p. 375; 20, p. 3365; 21, p. 3009; 22, p. 1547; 23, p. 1430; 25, p. 18; 27, p. 524.

Haematein.

Haematein occurs in the "blue wood" of *Haematoxylon campechianum,* forming the characteristic pigment of the logwood dye stuffs. It crystallizes in microscopic crystals of a reddish brown color with a yellowish green metallic reflection. It is very slightly soluble in water, difficultly soluble in alcohol, ether, and acetic acid, insoluble in chloroform and benzene. It is soluble in alkaline solutions, in sodium hydroxide with a bright red and in ammonia with a violet red color. It dyes fabrics mordanted with aluminum a grayish blue to black color; with iron, black; with chromium, blue black; with copper, greenish black and with tin, a violet color.

Literature on Haematein.

Baeyer, — Ber., 4, p. 457.
Erdmann, — Ann., 44, p. 294; 216, p. 236.
Halberstadt, — B., 14, p. 611.
Hesse, — Ann., 109, p. 337.
Mayer, — Chem. Centralbl., 1904, I. p. 228.
Perkin, — Ber., 15, p. 2337; Jr. Chem. Soc., 41, p. 368; 93, p. 1115; 95, p. 381.

PIGMENTS REFERABLE TO HYDROCARBONS OF THE DEGREE OF SATURATION C_nH_{2n-18}.

There occur in plants pigments referable to four hydrocarbons of four distinct structural configurations, falling under this degree of saturation, as follows:

I. Nine double bonds and one cycle.
The chlorophylls.
II. Eight double bonds and two cycles.
Pigments referable to diphenyl-1, 7-heptadiene-1, 6.
III. Seven double bonds and three cycles.
Pigments referable to phenyl-dihydronaphthalene.
IV. Six double bonds and four cycles.
Pigments referable to anthracene.

With the exception of the first configuration under which we find the two chlorophylls chlorophyll-a and chlorophyll-b, so far as is known only one pigment under each structural configuration has been isolated. These are II. Curcumin, III. Trifoletin, IV. Chrysarobin.

I. PIGMENTS REFERABLE TO HYDROCARBONS OF THE CONFIGURATION NINE DOUBLE BONDS AND ONE CYCLE.

The Chlorophylls.

The chemistry of chlorophyll has attracted more attention and has been the subject of more investigations than that of any other plant pigment. This is due not only to the extremely wide distribution and abundant occurrence of chlorophyll in plants but also to its physiological importance and the role which it appears to play in photosynthesis. Notwithstanding, however, the abundance of material available, the importance of the problem and the attention paid to it, up until quite recently, but little light has been thrown upon the subject and even now the chemistry of chlorophyll is far from being elucidated.

It is not at all the purpose of this paper to discuss the complex chemistry of chlorophyll, nor is this necessary in view of the very thorough revision of the subject by Marchlewski,[1] published in 1909, and the yet more recent one by Willstaetter[2] in 1913. A brief mention of the subject, however, is not out of place and seems desirable in order to place chlorophyll in its class among the plant pigments.

Chlorophyll, according to Willstaetter, is a complex magnesium compound, or rather, a mixture of at least two such complex compounds, the blue green chlorophyll-a, $C_{55}H_{72}O_5N_4Mg$, and the yellow green chlorophyll-b, $C_{55}H_{70}O_6N_4Mg$.

Both of these chlorophylls are esters of phytol, which is a constant constituent of chlorophyll. Phytol is an open chain primary alcohol of the formula of saturation C_nH_{2n}. The following structural formula has been suggested for phytol:

$$\begin{array}{ccccccccccc} CH_3 - & CH - & CH - & CH - & CH - & CH - & CH - & CH - & C = & C - & CH_2\,OH \\ & | & | & | & | & | & | & | & | & | & \\ & CH_3 & CH_3 & CH_3 & CH_3 & CH_3 & CH_3 & CH_3 & CH_3 & CH_3 & \end{array}$$

Making it, according to the Geneva Congress system of nomenclature, nonamethyl-2, 3, 4, 5, 6, 7, 8, 9, 10-undecene-2-ol-1.

By the action of an enzyme, chlorophyllase, chlorophyll-a is hydrolised yielding phytol and chlorophyllid-a

$C_{20}H_{39}OH$	$MgN_4C_{32}H_{30}OCOOCH_3COOH$
Phytol	Chlorophyllid-a

while chlorophyll-b yields phytol and chlorophyllid-b.

$C_{20}H_{39}OH$	$MgN_4C_{32}H_{28}O_2COOCH_3COOH$
Phytol	Chlorophyllid-b

Phytol is a non-colored substance and appears to play no direct part in pigmentation.

---

[1] Die Chemie der Chlorophylle Braunschweig, 1909.

[2] Untersuchungen ueber Chlorophyll, Berlin, 1913.

Chlorophyllid-a and chlorophyllid-b, heated with caustic alkalies, after passing through a number of intermediate stages, both yield aetiophyllin, $C_{31}H_{34}N_4Mg$, which appears to be the basic colored portion of the molecule. For aetiophyllin Willstaetter has suggested the following structural formula:

```
                                                          CH ═══ CH
                                                          |       |
 I₃ ──── C ────── CH                                      C ───── C
         ║          \\                                  //        |
         ║            N                              N            |
         ║          /   `.                         .' \           |
 H₃ ──── C ────── C       `.                     .'     C ────── CH
                   \\       `.                 .'     //
                     C ──────────────────────────── -C
                    /          `.           .'         \
 H₃ ──── C ══════ C              `.       .'            C ═══ C ──── (
         |         \\              `.   .'            //      |
         |           N ─────────── Mg ─────────── N           |
         |          /                                 \       |
         C ══════ C                                     C ═══ C ──── (
                  |                                     |
                 CH₃                                   CH₃
```

Referring aetiophyllin, as represented above, to the underlying hydrocarbon it is found to be derived from $C_{31}H_{44}$, a duodecatetrene derivative with six side chains, and falling under the formula of saturation C_nH_{n2-18} as below.

```
CH₃—CH=C—C = CH— C ———C—CH = C—C = CH—CH₃
        |  |       ||       ||          |   |
      CH₃ CH₂      CH       CH        CH₂ CH₃
           |        |        |          |
         CH₃ CH₃CH₂C        CH         CH₃
                    ||       ||
                  CH₂C       C -- CH₂
                    |        |     |
                   CH₃       HC=CH
```

Aetiophyll itself is the product of the deammoniation and combination with magnesium, of a decamido substitution product of the above hydrocarbon.

```
                              H
                             /NH2
                            C-NH.CH=CH
                            |    |  | /NH2
                     CH3 C       C—C
                         ||      ||   \NH2
                 CH3 CH2 C       CH          CH3
          CH3
           |             |       |           |
NH2  CH3  CH2  NH2       C NH2   C NH2 NH2 CH2 CH3 NH3
 |    |    |    |        ||      ||   |    |    |    |
CH3—C = C—C = C————————C——————C————C = C—C = C—CH3
```

By deammoniation of the above compound and subsequent substitution of magnesium for imido hydrogen aetiophyllin would be formed.

II. Pigments referable to hydrocarbons of the configuration eight double bonds and two cycles.

Pigments referable to diphenyl- 1, 7 -heptadiene- 1, 6.

```
                                        CH  CH
      CH2 —— CH ══ CH. —— C<          >CH
     /                                  CH  CH
CH2
     \                                  CH  CH
      CH2 —— CH ══ CH —— C<           >CH
                                        CH  CH
```

Diphenyl-1, 7-heptadiene-1, 6

```
        O                               CH   COCH3
       //
      C —— CH ══ CH —— C<               >COH
     /                                  CH  CH
CH2
     \                                  CH  CH
      C —— CH ══ CH —— C<               >COH
       \\
        O                               CH   COCH3
```

Curcumine

Curcumine occurs in the rhizom of *Curcuma longa, C. viridiflora,* and probably in other species of *Zingiberaceae.* It was first obtained in the crystalline form by Daube,[1] in 1870, though it had been studied by Vogel and Pelletier[2] as early as 1815. In 1881 Jackson and Menke[3] made the first correct analysis of curcumine and ascribed to it the formula $C_{14}H_{14}O_4$. After making an extended study of its reactions they ascribed to it the structural formula,-

CH COOH CH
HC C—CH—C CH
HOC CH HC CH
COH CH

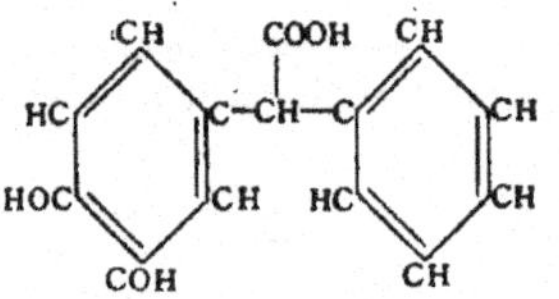

This formula was accepted until 1897 when Ciamician and Silber[4] concluded that the molecule contained two hydroxy and two methoxy groups and should be represented by the formula $C_{21}H_{20}O_6$ instead of $C_{14}H_{14}O_4$. Molecular weight determinations made by Perkin[5] and his associates in 1904 sustained the conclusion of Ciamician and Silber. Jackson and Clarke,[6] in 1905–1908, made another examination which they interpreted as proving the correctness of Jackson's earlier formula. In 1910 Milobendzki, Kostanecki, and Lampe[7] by a series of syntheses proved the correctness of Camician and Silber's formula, assigning to the molecule the structural formula given above. In 1914 Jackson and Clarke[8] by further work confirmed this formula.

Curcumine crystallizes in orange yellow crystals with a bluish reflection, and a melting point of 178°. It is insoluble in water and ligroin, almost insoluble in benzene, somewhat soluble

[1] Ber., 3, p. 609.
[2] Jr. de Pharm., 50, p. 259.
[3] Ber., 14, p. 485; 15, p. 1761; 17, (Ref.) p. 332.
[4] Ber., 30, p. 192; Gazz. chim. ital., 27, I. p. 561.
[5] Jr. Chem. Soc., 85, p. 63.
[6] Ber., 38, p. 2712; 39, p. 3269; Am. Chem. Jr., 39, p. 699.
[7] Ber., 43, p. 2163.
[8] Am. Chem. Jr., 45, p. 48.

in cold alcohol, ether and carbon disulphide. The solution in ether gives a green fluorescence. Its reddish brown reaction is well known.

In the course of the various investigations of which curcumine has been the subject a large number of derivatives have been formed.

The more important of the many investigations of curcumine are given in the following list:

Literature on Curcumine.

Bolley, Suida and Daube, — Jr. prakt. Chem., 103, p. 474.
Ciamician and Silber, — B., 30, p. 192; Gazz. chim. ital., 27, I. p. 561.
Daube and Claus, — Jr. prakt. Chem., (2) 2, p. 86; B., 3, p. 609.
Iwanon, — Ber., 3, 624.
Jackson, — Ber., 14, 485.
Jackson and Mencke, — B., 15, 1761; Am. Chem. Jr., 4, 368.
Jackson and Mencke, — Pharm. Jr. Trans. III. 13, 839.
Jackson and Mencke, — Ber., (Ref.) 17, 332.
Jackson and Warren, — Am. Chem. Jr., 18, 111.
Jackson and Clarke, — Ber., 38, 2712.
Jackson and Clarke, — Ber., 39, 2269.
Jackson and Clarke, — Am. Chem. Jr., 39, 699.
Jackson and Clarke, — Am. Chem. Jr., 45, 48.
Kachler, — B., 3, 713.
Leach, — Jr. Chem. Soc., 26, 1210.
LePage, — Arch. Pharm. (2) 97, 240.
Milobendzki, Kostanecki and Lampe, — Ber., 43, 2163.
Perkin, — Jr. Chem. Soc., 85, 63.
Rupe, — Ber., 40, 4909.
Thompson, — Pharm. Jr. Trans. 23.
Vogel and Pelletier, — Jr. de Pharm., 50, 259.
Vogel, — Ann., 44, 297, B. Repert. Pharm., 27, 274.

III. PIGMENTS REFERABLE TO HYDROCARBONS OF THE CONFIGURATION SEVEN DOUBLE BONDS AND THREE CYCLES.

Pigments referable to phenyl- dihydronaphthalene.

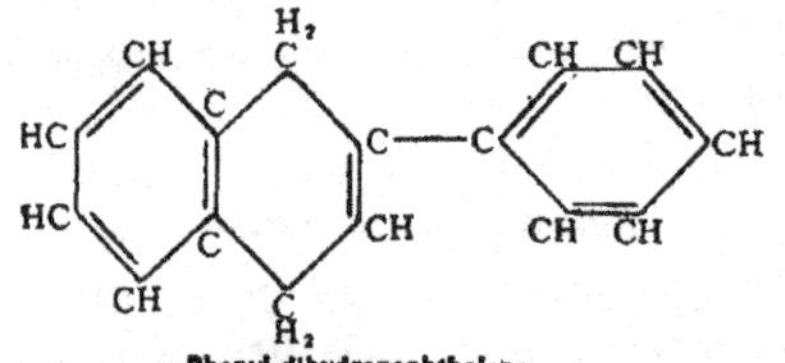

Phenyl-dihydronaphthalene

One pigment apparently a derivative of the above hydrocarbon has been isolated from plants. This is trifolitin, probably a tetrahydroxy derivative of phenyl-naphthaquinone.

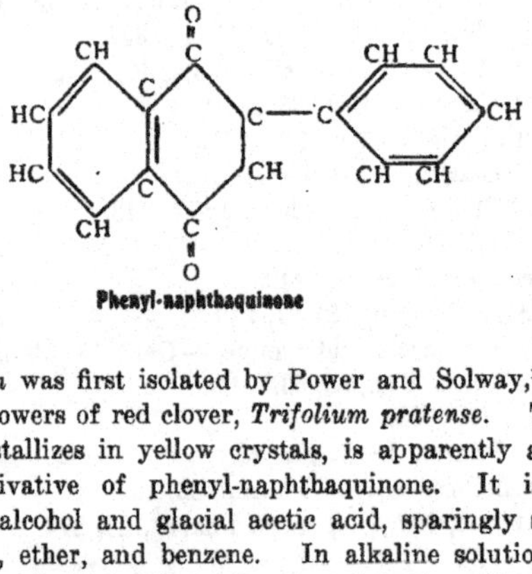

Phenyl-naphthaquinone

Trifolitin was first isolated by Power and Solway,[1] in 1910, from the flowers of red clover, *Trifolium pratense.* Trifolitin, which crystallizes in yellow crystals, is apparently a tetrahydroxy derivative of phenyl-naphthaquinone. It is readily soluble in alcohol and glacial acetic acid, sparingly soluble in chloroform, ether, and benzene. In alkaline solutions it dissolves with a bright yellow color, in sulphuric acid with a yellow color. It dyes mordanted cotton a bright yellow.

[1] Jr. Chem. Soc., 97, 241.

IV. Pigments referable to hydrocarbons of the configuration six double bonds and four cycles.

Pigments referable to methyl-anthracene.

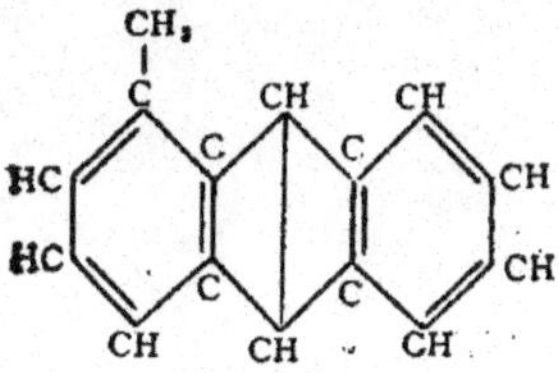

Methyl Anthracene

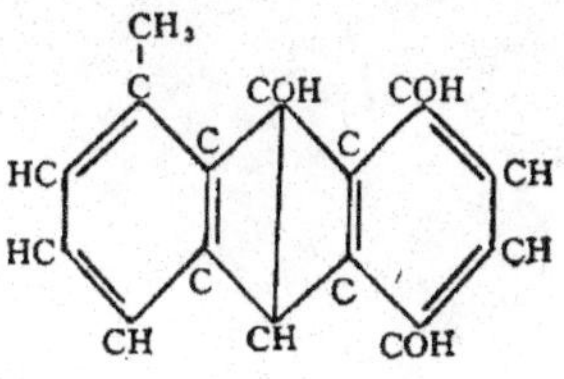

Chrysarobin

Chrysarobin[1]—a trihydroxy derivative of methyl-anthracene occurs along with dichrysarobin, dichrysarobin methyl ether and another similar substance $C_{17}H_{18}O_4$ in Goa powder, obtained from *Andira araroba*,[2] also along with chrysophanic acid and emodin in *Rhamnus purshiana*.[3]

Chrysarobin and chrysophanic acid were formerly thought to be identical but the work of Hesse[4] and later that of Jowett and Potter[5] have shown the latter to be a derivative of methyl anthraquinone, while the former is a derivative of methyl anthracene. Chrysorobin is however readily oxidized to chrysophanic acid.

Chrysorobin crystallizes in small yellow tabular crystals and needles. It melts at 177°. It is easily soluble in chloroform, acetic acid and benzene, more difficultly soluble in alcohol and ether. It is insoluble in water and ammonia but soluble in sulphuric acid with a yellow color, insoluble in very dilute potassium hydroxide but soluble in a stronger solution with a yellow color. Upon exposure to the air in alkaline solution it goes to chrysophanic acid.

---

[1] Jr. Chem. Soc., 81, p. 1575.
[2] Ber., 11, p. 1603; Ann., 309, p. 32; Pharm. Jr., 5, p. 721.
[3] Proc. Am. Pharm. Assoc., 52, p. 288 (1904).
[4] Ann., 301, p. 82.
[5] Jr. Chem. Soc., 81, p. 1578; 83, p. 1327.

CPSIA information can be obtained
at www.ICGtesting.com
Printed in the USA
BVOW03s0433241217
503569BV00001B/44/P